Jewish
Information
Quiz Book

ALFRED J. KOLATCH

jD | JONATHAN DAVID PUBLISHERS
MIDDLE VILLAGE, N.Y. 11379

JEWISH INFORMATION QUIZ BOOK
Copyright 1967, 1980

by
ALFRED J. KOLATCH

JONATHAN DAVID PUBLISHERS, INC.
68-22 Eliot Avenue
Middle Village, NY 11379

REVISED EDITION, 1980

This is a reprint edition distributed by Bookthrift, New York. Bookthrift is a registered trademark of Simon & Schuster, Inc.

ISBN 0-671-07539-X

Library of Congress Catalog Card No. 66-30508

Printed in the United States of America

CONTENTS

QUESTIONS

ANSWERS

Part I – PERSONS AND PLACES

1. This prominent American statesman served as a U.S. Senator (1949-1957) and as Governor of New York (1928-32). He was the first director-general of the United Nations Relief and Rehabilitation Agency (1943-1946). His name is

    a. Jacob K. Javits
    b. Emanuel Celler
    c. Herbert H. Lehman

2. One of the first Jews to arrive in New Amsterdam (New York) in 1654 was a Levy. He fought for the right of Jews to have full citizenship. His full name is

    a. Aaron Levy
    b. Reuben Levy
    c. Asser Levy

3. Lithuanian-born, Abraham Mapu (1808-1867), was a well-known figure in the 19th century because he was the first person to

    a. discover a cure for rabies
    b. compose a Jewish national anthem
    c. write a Hebrew novel

4. A famous United States Army soldier, who graduated from West Point and served in World War II with distinction, went to Palestine in 1948 as military adviser to the Haganah. He was killed in action in Jerusalem during the war for independence. His name is

    a. Jacob Javits
    b. David Marcus
    c. Felix Frankfurter

5. The first of the famous Rothschild family was Mayor Amschel Rothschild, born in 1743. He had five sons who established themselves in five European centers. They became famous as

    a. financiers and philanthropists
    b. artists and musicians
    c. authors and poets

6. A German philosopher, born in 1886 of an assimilated family, was on the verge of embracing Christianity when he had a sudden change of heart as a result of his attendance at an orthodox Yom Kippur service in 1913. His name is

    a. Franz Werfel
    b. Franz Rosensweig
    c. Sigmund Freud

7. In 1903, the British offered Theodore Herzl a portion of territory in their colony of Kenya,

in Africa, where Jews might come and settle. This proposal was rejected by the seventh Zionist Congress in 1905, after Herzl's death. The scheme became known as the

    a. Uganda Scheme
    b. Balfour Declaration
    c. White Paper

8. Born in 1867, this woman was a dedicated social worker. In 1893 she founded the Henry Street Settlement in New York and was its director until 1933. She also organized the first non-sectarian public health nursing system and the first public school nursing system. She died in 1940. Her name is

    a. Golda Meir
    b. Henrietta Szold
    c. Lillian D. Wald

9. Chaim Weizmann was born in 1874 in Russia, and died in Israel in 1952. In 1948 he was elected the first President of the State of Israel. Although much of his life was devoted to Zionism, by profession he was a

    a. physician
    b. lawyer
    c. chemist

10. Treblinka, in Poland, was the site of a camp that gained renown in 1942 and 1943. It was a

    a. U.S. military reservation
    b. Russian evacuation center
    c. Nazi extermination camp

11. Saul (Shaul) Tschernichovsky was born in the Crimea in 1875, and died in Palestine in 1943. He was a physician by profession but gained his fame as a

    a. poet
    b. scientist
    c. dancer

12. Menahem Mendel Ussishkin, who was born in 1863 and died in 1941, was an outstanding

    a. scientist
    b. Zionist
    c. philanthropist

13. Judah Touro was born in the United States in 1775. He became a wealthy merchant and helped George Washington financially during the American Revolution. In his home town a synagogue, known by his name, still stands

and has become a national shrine. In what city and state is the Touro Synagogue?

a. New Orleans, Louisiana
b. Newport, Rhode Island
c. Alexandria, Virginia

14. Titus, the mighty emperor, who was the son of Vespasian, destroyed the Second Temple in Jerusalem in the year 70. He was a

a. Roman
b. Persian
c. Babylonian

15. After the death of Chaim Weizmann in 1952, a candidate was invited to run for election as the President of Israel. He refused, preferring to stay on at Princeton University where he could pursue his studies in physics. He continued to show great interest in Israel and donated his manuscripts on the theory of relativity to the Hebrew University. His name is

a. Albert Einstein
b. Sigmund Freud
c. Jonas Salk

16. Thomas de Torquemada was a 15th century Dominican who was appointed to be Grand Inquisitor of his country. He was largely re-

sponsible for the expulsion of the Jews from his
country in 1492. What country was it?

    a. France
    b. Spain
    3. Italy

17. After the Babylonian exile ended (around
510 B.C.E.) most Jews returned to Palestine
with the consent of Cyrus, King of Persia. One
of the first Jews to return was

    a. Zerubabel
    b. Akiba
    c. Maimonides

18. An Israeli soldier, who served as Chief of
Staff of the Israeli Army from 1949-52, became
a Professor of Archaeology at the Hebrew University in 1959, and published books on the Dead
Sea Scrolls. His name is

    a. Yigael Yadin
    b. Yalkut Shimoni
    c. Julian Morgenstern

19. This electrical engineer of German birth
(1865) came to the United States in 1889. He
taught at Union College in Schenectady, N. Y.,

and was for many years chief consulting engineer of the General Electric Co. His name is

    a. Thomas Edison
    b. Lewis Strauss
    c. Charles Steinmetz

20. The Sinai Operation came to a close on
March 1, 1957 when

    a. Professor Sukenik of the Hebrew Uni-
       versity announced the discovery of the
       Dead Sea Scrolls.
    b. All patients at the Hadassah Hospital
       were granted free medical treatment.
    c. Israel announced its intention to with-
       draw its troops from the Gaza Strip.

21. The Arch of Titus, which depicts the god-
dess of victory crowning Titus, and also the
march of Jewish captives carrying the Temple
vessels after the destruction of the Second Temple in the year 70, can be seen in what city?

    a. Jerusalem
    b. Alexandria
    c. Rome

22. Stern is a popular name used by Jews.
Avraham Stern (born, 1907), Isaac Stern
(born, 1920), and Otto Stern (born, 1888) are

three famous Sterns who achieved distinction in various fields. Match the above with their achievements. Which one was

a. a leader of the Palestine underground fighters in the 1940's known as the Stern Gang.
b. an American violinist virtuoso.
c. a 1943 Nobel Prize winner for his achievements in physics.

23. This archaeologist was born in Poland in 1889 and settled in Palestine in 1912. He taught at the Hebrew University from 1935 until his death in 1953. In 1947 he realized the importance of the Dead Sea Scrolls and acquired several specimens for the Hebrew University. His name is

a. Chaim Weizmann
b. Ben Gurion
c. Eliezer Sukenik

24. An American nuclear expert, born in 1900, was an Admiral in the U.S. Navy and was responsible for the launching of the world's first atomic submarine. His name is

a. Mickey Marcus
b. Walter Shirra
c. Hyman George Rickover

25. After Joseph died, a new king became ruler over Egypt. The Israelites were forced into labor gangs and were treated cruelly. Among the things they built were two storage cities. What were the names of the cities?

    a. Sodom and Gomorrah
    b. Pithom and Raamses
    c. Gad and Asher

26. Abraham Soyer, an author and Hebrew pedagogue who taught at the Teacher's Institute of Yeshiva University until his death in 1940, was the father of Isaac and Raphael Soyer. Both sons became noted

    a. teachers
    b. doctors
    c. artists

27. A world-famous 17th century Dutch-born philosopher came from a family of Portuguese Marranos. His unorthodox religious views led to his excommunication by the Sephardic community in 1656. His name is

    a. Baruch Spinoza
    b. Hasdai Crescas
    c. Joseph Caro

28. These three men have occupied high political office in their respective states. Which two served as Governor of their state?

  a. Jacob Javits of New York
  b. Moses Alexander of Idaho
  c. Arthur Seligman of New Mexico

29. Solomon Schechter was born in Rumania in 1850 but studied in Vienna and Berlin. In 1890, he was named Lecturer in Talmud at Cambridge in England, and in 1901 was appointed President of the Jewish Theological Seminary of America. In 1896 and 1897, he spent a great deal of time working on the Geniza fragments. In what city were these fragments located?

  a. Paris
  b. London
  c. Cairo

30. A famous immunologist, born in Hungary in 1877, discovered the test that is able to determine one's susceptibility to diphtheria. His name is

  a. Bela Schick
  b. Jacob Schiff
  c. Jonas Salk

31. Ilya Schor was born in Poland in 1904. He studied in Warsaw and Paris before settling in the United States in 1941. He is a well-known

    a. author and journalist
    b. artist and silversmith
    c. music conductor and composer

32. In 17th and 18th century Germany, Jews who were given special privileges and were allowed to travel freely because they were favored by various rulers were called

    a. *schutzjuden*
    b. *hofjuden*
    c. *hochjuden*

33. Louis Dembitz Brandeis was born in Louisville, Kentucky, in 1856, and died in 1941. He was a leading American Zionist and a prominent member of the bar. Brandeis University, in Waltham, Mass., was so-called in his honor. He was the first Jew ever to be appointed to the Supreme Court. The president who appointed him was

    a. Woodrow Wilson in 1916
    b. Howard B. Taft in 1910
    c. Franklin D. Roosevelt in 1934

34. Amos, Zechariah and Rashi are famous names in Jewish history. Two of them were prophets who are mentioned in the Bible. The other was a

    a. newspaper reporter
    b. musician
    c. Bible commentator

35. Which of these people lived first?

    a. Akiba
    b. Rashi
    c. Jonah
    d. Maimonides
    e. Josephus

36. A financier and American patriot who came to the United States from Poland in 1772, helped to finance the American revolution. His name is

    a. Jacob H. Schiff
    b. Baron Edmond de Rothschild
    c. Haym Salomon

37. Jonas Salk, born in 1914, was professor of bacteriology at the University of Pittsburgh from 1949-61, and since 1961 has headed the Institute for Biological Research at the University of California. He was awarded the Nobel

Prize because of his discovery of a vaccine which prevents

a. diabetes
b. polio
c. measles

38. Rabbi Solomon ben Isaac (1040-1105), who is also called Rabbi Shlomo Yitzchaki, wrote commentaries on the Bible and Talmud which are studied to this day. In what country did he live?

a. North Africa
b. Germany
c. France

39. A Babylonian city situated on the Euphrates was an important center of Jewish culture from the third to the eleventh centuries. The first great academy of Jewish learning was established there by Judah ben Ezekiel, and many great talmudic scholars conducted classes and gave lectures there. The name of the city was

a. Barcelona
b. Pumbedita
c. Provence

40. Martin Luther, the man who inspired the Protestant Reformation in the 16th century, objected to both the vices and the authoritarianism of the Catholic Church. As a result of Luther's revolution, tolerance towards the Jews in Germany

   a. became worse
   b. remained the same
   c. was vastly improved

41. Uriah Phillip Levy (1792-1862) was an American naval officer. The great achievement he is credited with is the

   a. appointment of Jewish chaplains in the navy
   b. release from duty of Jewish sailors on Yom Kippur
   c. abolition of corporal punishment in the U.S. Navy

42. During the first century (between 6 and 66) the Roman emperors sent in their Governors to rule Judea. These Governors were called

   a. Hasmoneans
   b. Procurators
   c. Amoraim

43. The Middle Eastern state where Esther, the heroine of the Purim story, played an important role in the survival of the Jewish people was Persia. Today, about 75,000 Jews still live in this country, which goes by the name of

a. Iraq
b. Iran
c. Syria

44. A well-known leader of the Jews, Theodor Herzl, made the following statement about the aspirations of Jews towards the acquisition of a homeland. He said: "If you will it, it is no ———." What is the missing word?

a. dream
b. miracle
c. problem

45. Abraham Albert Michelson, Isaac Isidore Rabi, Emilio Segre and Niels Bohr gained fame for their discoveries in one particular field. They were all Jewish Nobel Prize winners because of their

a. achievements in physics
b. achievements in chemistry
c. achievements in literature

46. Nehardea was a city famous for its academy of learning. There, many scholars, whose

discussions are recorded in the Talmud, made
their homes. Samuel was the well-known princi-
pal of this academy in the 3rd century C.E. In
what country was Nehardea located?

    a. Egypt
    b. Palestine
    c. Babylonia

47. In talmudic times (first five centuries of
the present era) teachers delivered their lectures through an interpreter. The lecturer would
speak in a soft voice, and the interpreter would
repeat it in a loud voice, so all could hear. The
Aramaic name for this interpreter is

    a. *tanna*
    b. *amora*
    c. *meturgeman*

48. A French Jew, born in 1907, occupied
many appointed and elective offices in France
between 1932, when he was elected to the French
parliament, and 1956, when he served as vice-
premier under Mollet. From June, 1954, to
to February, 1955, he served as premier of
France. His name is

    a. Pierre Mendès-France
    b. Henri Louis Bergson
    c. Jean Benoit-Lèvy

49. The Earl of Beaconsfield was a British statesman who was born of Jewish parents in 1804. He died in 1881. When he was 13 his father had him baptized. From 1874 to 1880 he served as Prime Minister of England. His name is

    a. Alfred Dreyfus
    b. Benjamin Disraeli
    c. Lord Arthur Balfour

50. One of the greatest Jewish philosophers of all time was born in Cordova, Spain, in 1135. He died in 1170 and, according to tradition, was buried in Tiberias (Palestine), where his tomb attracts many visitors today. His famous work, *A Guide for the Perplexed*, has influenced not only Jews, but non-Jewish scholars including Thomas Aquinas, John Spencer and Gottfried Leibniz. This philosopher's name is

    a. Moses Maimonides
    b. Moses Nachmanides
    c. Moses Mendelssohn

51. On May 3, 1882, the Russian government enacted legislation which prohibited Jews from acquiring property in all parts of Russia except in certain towns called the Pale of Settlement.

These laws, which were legally revoked in March, 1917, were called the

    a. May Laws
    b. Blue Laws
    c. Jew Laws

52. In the past 100 years, many Jewish doctors have done significant pioneer work in medical research and have been responsible for many important discoveries. Here are three doctors who have made major contributions in 1) psychoanalysis 2) syphilis testing 3) bacteriology. Which of these doctors is the leading figure in each area?

    a. August von Wasserman
    b. Sigmund Freud
    c. Ferdinand Cohn

53. Golda Meir was born in Russia in 1898, but moved to the United States as a child. In 1921, she settled in Palestine. In 1948, she was sent to Russia as the first Israeli minister. Her original name was

    a. Golda Meyers
    b. Golda Meyerson
    c. Golda Meyerowitz

54. During the closing years of the 15th century in Spain and Portugal many Jews were forced to accept Christianity or lose their lives. Outwardly, they acted like Christians, but secretly, behind closed doors, they practiced Judaism. These Jews and their descendants were known as

    a. Pharisees
    b. Marranos
    c. Karaites

55. This German social philosopher was born of Jewish parents who abandoned Judaism before his birth in 1818. In 1848, together with Friedrich Engels, he wrote *The Communist Manifesto*, which ends with the words "Workers of the world unite!" His attitude towards Jews and Judaism was one of antipathy and contempt. His name is

    a. Alexander Marx
    b. Karl Heinrich Marx
    c. Adolf Bernhard Marx

56. This town in Poland, 30 miles west of Cracow, was the site of the largest Nazi exter-

mination camp during World War II. What was
its name?

    a. Auschwitz
    b. Augsburg
    c. Barcelona

57. Jewish scholars who lived in Palestine
and Babylonia from the third to the sixth centuries and whose opinions are recorded in the
Talmud are called

    a. Amoraim
    b. Pharisees
    c. Tosafists

58. In 1887, many Cuneiform tablets, reveal-
ing much of the early history of Egypt were
discovered on the site of the capital city of Egypt
which existed during the reign of Pharaoh
Amenhotep IV. What was the name of this site?

    a. Tel Aviv
    b. Tel Chai
    c. Tel El Amarna

59. An English financier who died in 1185 had
among his clients members of the nobility, as
well as religious leaders. With the funds he provided they built abbeys and cathedrals. Upon

his death, the Crown confiscated all his property. Who was he?

   a. Benjamin Disraeli
   b. Louis Dembitz Brandeis
   c. Aaron of Lincoln

60. Operation Magic Carpet was the name given to the rescue of a large number of Jews who were brought to Israel by airplane after the establishment of the State of Israel. Where did the Jews come from?

   a. They came from Germany
   b. They came from Poland
   c. They came from Yemen

61. Max Nordau, a Budapest-born Zionist leader once coined a German expression which described the type of rootless Jew who lived in Eastern Europe. This Jew had no regular, stable occupation and lived on peddling and petty speculation. The name used for such Jews was

   a. *luftmenschen*
   b. *chassidim*
   c. *hofjuden*

62. Many famous Jews were named Adler. One of these was a great psychologist, one was a great journalist, and one was a great Oriental

scholar and community leader. Which of these is correct?

    a. Alfred Adler (born 1870—died 1937), was a great psychologist

    b. Julius Ochs Adler (born 1892—died 1955), was a great Oriental scholar

    c. Cyrus Adler (born 1863—died 1940), was a great journalist

63. According to tradition, a famous rabbi, teacher and scholar, who was born about 40 C.E. and died about 135 C.E. in Palestine, left his wife and went off to begin his studies at the age of forty. His wife's name was Rachel and his father-in-law's name was Kalba Sabbua. What was his name?

    a. Akiba ben Joseph
    b. Judah the Prince
    c. Hillel the Elder

64. According to an old legend (which is not accurate) the King of Macedonia visited Jerusalem during his reign (336-323 B.C.E.). He was very friendly toward Jews. As a token of their appreciation, many Jews named their sons

born in that year by his name. What was the monarch's name?

    a. Josephus
    b. Aristotle
    c. Alexander

65. Arthur James Balfour was a British statesman who, on November 2, 1917, issued a statement that proved to be of vital importance to the future of

    a. the Jews in the English navy
    b. the State of Israel
    c. Jews who wanted to visit British colonies

66. This man is considered to be the first Jewish settler to arrive in New Amsterdam (New York). He arrived at least one month earlier than the first group of Jews who came from Brazil in 1654. What was his name?

    a. Salo Baron
    b. Jacob Barsimon
    c. Judah Touro

67. This man was born in 1870 and died in 1965. He was an important financier and public official. He was especially known as an adviser

to many U.S. presidents on economic matters.
His name is

   a. Billy Rose
   b. Arthur Goldberg
   c. Bernard Baruch

68. The first president of the State of Israel
was Chaim Weizmann, a chemist by profession.
Yitzhak Ben-Zvi was the second president. In
addition to his involvement in politics, Ben-Zvi
had gained a reputation as

   a. a journalist and scholar
   b. a doctor of medicine
   c. a farmer

69. The scholarly and saintly wife of Rabbi
Meir, in the 2nd century, was the only woman
mentioned in the Talmud who ever participated
in legal discussions. Her two children died on
the same day, the Sabbath, but she kept the fact
from her husband until after the Sabbath. What
was her name?

   a. Alexandra
   b. Beruria
   c. Rachel

70. This Swedish diplomat, who was born in
1895 and died in 1948, negotiated with the Ger-

mans at the end of World War II to rescue Jewish survivors. He was assassinated in Jerusalem in 1948 while serving as a United Nations' mediator in the Jewish-Arab conflict. His name is

    a. Count Folke Bernadotte
    b. Dag Hammarskjold
    c. Ingmar Johannsenn

71. According to the Book of Genesis, Noah's ark came to rest on Mount Ararat. In 1825, an American proposed that a place of refuge be established for Jews on Grand Island, which is in the Niagara River, northwest of Buffalo, N. Y. He proposed that the place be named Ararat. What was the man's name?

    a. Judah Touro
    b. Mordecai Manuel Noah
    c. Isaac Abravanel

72. Bethlehem is sacred to Christians because it is the birthplace of Jesus. To Jews, Bethlehem is significant because it is the birthplace of

    a. King David
    b. Ben-Gurion
    c. Chaim Nachman Bialik

73. In 1928, the Soviet government, at the suggestion of President Kalinin, allocated a portion of Eastern Siberia for the settlement of Jews. Yiddish was to be recognized as the official language. The name of that region is

a. Slabodka
b. Birobidjan
c. Minsk

74. Three outstanding personalities with the surname Bloch have made major contributions to American and Jewish life. Can you identify which contribution listed below applies to Ernest Bloch, which to Felix Bloch, and which to Joshua Bloch?

a. He served as the Jewish librarian at the New York Public Library from 1923 to 1956.
b. He served as Professor of Physics at Stanford University, and was the 1952 Nobel Prize winner for his work in nuclear magnetic fields.
c. He was the composer who wrote music for the synagogue service.

75. This philosopher, born in 1878 and died in 1965, was a professor at the Hebrew University. He was one of the greatest authorities on

Hasidism and had a great influence on the Christian world. His conception of religious faith was that it was a dialogue between man and God. His name is

    a. Franz Rosenzweig
    b. Franz Werfel
    c. Martin Buber

76. Buchenwald is a town in Germany about five miles northwest of Weimar. One of the reasons why this town became well-known was because, in 1937,

    a. the Weimar Republic was established there
    b. a new synagogue was built there
    c. the Nazis established a concentration camp there

77. Among the 319 Nobel Prize winners between the years 1901-1959 some were Jews. What is the total number of Jews who won the Award during this period?

    a. 10
    b. 40
    c. 80

78. The land that is today called Israel was called in the days of Moses

    a. Canaan
    b. Ur
    c. Sinai

79. The Ezra synagogue was built in Cairo, Egypt, in 882. In 1896 a large deposit of sacred objects was discovered there. The most important articles found were

    a. old books
    b. silver candlesticks
    c. gold wine goblets

80. David Moses Cassuto was a scholar, rabbi and historian. He was born in 1883 in Florence, Italy, and died in 1951 in Jerusalem. He was a professor at the Hebrew University from 1939 until his death. He is best known for his writings in the field of

    a. mathematics
    b. history
    c. Bible

81. During World War II, four heroic chaplains lost their lives when their troopship was sunk. One of the four chaplains was a rabbi:

Rabbi Alexander Goode. What was the name of the troopship?

    a. SS Dorchester
    b. SS Eisenhower
    c. SS Shalom

82. In 1648, Bogdan Chmielnicki, a Polish patriot, conducted a campaign in which hundreds of Jewish communities were affected. The results of his efforts were known as

    a. the Chmielnicki land-reforms
    b. the Chmielnicki massacres
    c. the Chmielnicki Peace Conference

83. It was once believed that five members of the crew of Christopher Columbus were Jewish. Recent research has proven that only one, Columbus' interpreter, was undoubtedly Jewish. His name is

    a. Solomon ibn Gabirol
    b. Luis de Torres
    c. Solomon ben Maimon

84. Oliver Cromwell, Lord Protector of England from 1653-1658, was sympathetic toward the Jews. He supported the re-admission of Jews to England. The prominent Dutch rabbi who

visited Cromwell in 1655 to promote the re-
admission of Jews was

    a. Solomon ibn Gabirol
    b. Jehuda Halevi
    c. Manasseh ben Israel

85. Two cities in modern Israel play an important role in biblical history and represent her
furthest northern and southern geographical
points. Dan is the name of the northern city. The
name of the southern city is

    a. Jerusalem
    b. Haifa
    c. Beersheba

86. One of the great scholars of the first century B.C.E. is credited with the authorship of
the Golden Rule in its negative form. He said,
"Do unto others that which you would have
others do unto you." The name of this scholar is

    a. Akiba
    b. Judah
    c. Hillel

87. A former Governor of Connecticut (from
1955) was appointed Secretary of Health, Education and Welfare in 1961 by President Kennedy.

Later, he was elected to the Senate. His name is

a. Abraham Ribicoff
b. Jacob Javits
c. Seymour Halpern

88. A Chicago-born (1908) labor leader, the youngest child of a Russian immigrant, served in American government at different times, as Secretary of Labor, U.S. Supreme Court Justice, and U.S. Ambassador to the United Nations. His name is

a. Felix Frankfurter
b. Arthur Joseph Goldberg
c. Abraham A. Ribicoff

89. Ahad Ha-am (1856-1927) was one of the great Jewish essayists and philosophers of the past century. He was born in the Ukraine but spent most of his life in Odessa where he settled in 1886. His influence on many of the early Zionist leaders was considerable. Ahad Ha-am was his pen-name. His real name was

a. Asher Ginsberg
b. Louis Ginzberg
c. Jekuthiel Ginsburg

90. The president of the Hebrew Union College since 1947 (in 1950 it merged with the Jewish Institute of Religion) is Nelson Glueck. He achieved fame, prior to becoming the head of the seminary, as

    a. a great historian
    b. a Bible scholar who discovered the Cairo Geniza
    c. an archaeologist who discovered King Solomon's mines at Etzion Geber

91. There were many famous Jewish personalities named Gordon. Aharon David Gordon (1856-1922) was an outstanding Zionist philosopher. Judah Loeb Gordon (1830-1892), known as *Yalag*, was a great Hebrew poet. Who was Samuel Loeb Gordon (1867-1933), often referred to as *Shelag?*

    a. a Hebrew author and Bible commentator
    b. a Nobel prize winner for his work in physics
    c. a convert to Judaism who served in the English parliament

92. Jacob Frank, Sabbatai Zevi, David Alroy, Avraham Abulafia and Solomon Molcho lived in

different countries during the Middle Ages. They had one thing in common. They were all

    a. great physicians
    b. famous artists
    c. false messiahs

93. An Israeli diplomat who was born in Capetown, South Africa, in 1915, has served as a member of the Jewish Agency delegation to the United Nations in 1947. He also represented Israel at the U.N. from 1948 to 1959, and was Israeli ambassador to the U.S. from 1950 to 1959. In 1960, he became minister of education and culture in Israel. His name is

    a. Chaim Weizmann
    b. Emanuel Neumann
    c. Abba Eban

94. The founder of psychoanalysis was born in Vienna in 1856 and died in London in 1939. He had escaped to England in 1933, fleeing the Nazis. He considered all religion, including Judaism, as an irrational manifestation of the human mind, to be treated like any of the other neuroses. In the year of his death, his book entitled *Moses and Monotheism* appeared, in which

he attempted to prove that Moses was an Egyptian. His name is

   a. Carl Jung
   b. Moses Hess
   c. Sigmund Freud

95. Born in 1882, this great liberal served as an Associate Justice of the U.S. Supreme Court from 1939 until his death in 1965. From 1914 to 1939 he was a professor at the Harvard Law School. He was actively interested in the Zionist Organization as early as 1919 when he served as legal advisor to the Zionist delegation at the Paris Peace Conference. His name is

   a. Stephen S. Wise
   b. Felix Frankfurter
   c. Arthur Goldberg

96. The Marranos of Spain and Portugal, the Chuetas of Majorca, the Jedid-al-Islam in Persia, and the Neofiti of Southern Italy were all Crypto-Jews and had one thing in common. They all

   a. observed Passover two weeks after the regular date
   b. did not observe Yom Kippur as a day of fasting
   c. professed another religion outwardly, but practiced Judaism secretly

97. The Nobel Prizes were established from a fund of about $9,000,000 left by Alfred Nobel, the Swedish millionaire and inventor of dynamite. He died in 1896. Prizes were to be awarded in five fields of excellence: 1) physics 2) chemistry 3) physiology 4) literature 5) world peace. Quite a few Jews have won prizes through the years. In what fields did they excel the most?

   a. medicine, first; physics, second
   b. world peace, first; literature, second
   c. medicine, first; chemistry, second

98. One of the founders of the American Labor Party and the Jewish Labor Committee was born in Poland in 1892. He came to the United States in 1911. From 1932 to 1966 he was president of the International Ladies' Garment Workers' Union. During most of that time he was also Vice-president of the American Federation of Labor. He has been an important influence in local and national political life. His name is

   a. David Dubinsky
   b. David Merrick
   c. Arthur Goldberg

99. A college was opened in Philadelphia in 1909 to teach Bible and Rabbinics. Shortly after-

wards, a department for the teaching of Hebrew and cognate languages was added. Funds for the establishment of the school were provided under the will of a Philadelphia lawyer whose father was Jewish and whose mother was Christian. At the age of 14 the boy accepted Judaism and remained a devout Jew. His name is

    a. Abraham A. Neuman
    b. Moses Aaron Dropsie
    c. Mordecai Manuel Noah

100. This Jewish leader of Russian birth (1880-1940) insisted, as far back as 1918 that Jewish self-defense units be established in Palestine. He was the organizer of the militant Revisionist Zionist Organization. He was a prolific writer, having written poetry and novels. His name is

    a. Theodore Herzl
    b. Moses Hess
    c. Vladimir Jabotinsky

101. This scholar, born in Poland in 1876, and educated in Germany, was Professor of Biblical Literature at the Jewish Theological Seminary. He translated Dubnow's *History of the Jews in Russia and Poland* into English. In 1920, while on a relief mission in behalf of the American

Joint Distribution Committee, he was murdered by bandits in the Ukraine. His name is

a. Israel Friedlaender
b. Moses Hyamson
c. Solomon Schechter

102. Two men named Lewisohn are well known for their contributions to society. Adolph Lewisohn (1849-1938) was an American philanthropist who donated Lewisohn Stadium to the College of the City of New York. Ludwig Lewisohn (1883-1955) achieved fame as

a. an atomic scientist
b. a basketball player
c. professor and author

103. Many of the cities on the West Bank of Israel were famous biblical cities. Which of these cities is a West Bank city mentioned in the Bible?

a. Jerusalem
b. Jericho
c. Haifa

104. Of all the Israeli Prime Ministers, only one was a *sabra* (born in Israel). His name is

a. Menachem Begin
b. David Ben-Gurion
c. Yitzhak Rabin

105. Of all the Prime Ministers who served Israel only one was a woman. Her last name, before she changed it, was
   a. Myerson
   b. Meirowitz
   c. it was always Meir

106. After one of the four wars in which Israel was involved, a president of the United States pressured the Israelis to return the territory they had captured. The name of that president is
   a. Harry S. Truman
   b. Dwight D. Eisenhower
   c. Lyndon B. Johnson

107. A famous mountain located near Nablus is called Har (Mount) Gerizim. In the Bible it is called The Mountain of Blessing. A group that still follows many biblical Jewish practices celebrates many holidays on top of the mountain. The name of this group is
   a. the Kabbalists
   b. the Karaites
   c. the Samaritans

108. On March 26, 1979 a peace treaty was signed in Washington, D.C., between Israel and Egypt. The details of the treaty were hammered out at a Camp David, Maryland, summit conference. The most important people at that

meeting were
- a. Begin, Sadat, and Kissinger
- b. Weizmann, Sadat, and Vance
- c. Sadat, Begin, and Carter

109. The name by which the Jewish community in Israel was known, particularly in the years prior to 1948, was
- a. *Yishuv*
- b. *Yeshiva*
- c. *Yeshurun*

110. The Jews of Ethiopia have lived in that country for about 2,000 years. The name by which they are known in Jewish history is
- a. Zealots
- b. Samaritans
- c. Falashas

111. The mountain on which Moses received the Ten Commandments is called Mount Sinai. At the base of the mountain a religious institution was established many centuries ago. It is a
- a. yeshiva and synagogue
- b. a mosque
- c. a Catholic monastery

112. Pernambuco is a city in Brazil from which the first Jews to North America came in the year
- a. 1654
- b. 1754

   c. 1854.

113. Spinoza was a great Jewish philosopher who lived in Holland. One of the things that happened to him because of his teachings was that
   a. he was given the key to the city
   b. a boulevard in Amsterdam was named after him
   c. he was excommunicated by the Jewish community

114. On the very spot on which the Temple of Solomon stood, there now stands
   a. a Moslem mosque called Dome of the Rock
   b. a Christian church called Santa Caterina
   c. a Jewish synagogue called Temple Emanuel

115. St. Louis is a well-known city in Missouri. During World War II it was also the name of a
   a. U.S. battleship that was sunk at Pearl Harbor
   b. boat carrying refugees that was not permitted to land anywhere and was forced to return to Europe
   c. Catholic priest who saved the lives of many Jews and who helped them find a home in Palestine

116. Dayan, Maimonides, Mendelssohn—what did these famous personalities have in common?
    a. They had the same first name.
    b. They were born in 1916.
    c. They were army generals.

117. The 6,000,000 Jews who were murdered by the Nazis during World War II were imprisoned in more than 12 concentration camps in Germany, Poland, and Czechoslovakia. The most famous camps were
    a. Auschwitz and Bergen-Belsen
    b. Auschwitz and Berlin
    c. Theresienstat and Prague

118. The Touro Synagogue was named in honor of Judah Touro, a Jew who helped George Washington finance the war against the British. The Touro Synagogue, now a national shrine, is located in
    a. New York City
    b. Philadelphia, Pennsylvania
    c. Newport, Rhode Island

119. On Masada, overlooking the Dead Sea in southern Palestine, a Jewish king built a magnificent palace. In the year 73 C.E., after holding out for three years against the Romans, almost 1,000 zealots committed mass suicide rather than fall into Roman hands. The king who built the palace

on Masada was
   a. Herod
   b. Saul
   c. Solomon

120. The Inquisition started in fifteenth-century Spain and continued for more than a century. It was started in 1483 by Thomas de Torquemada, the confessor of Queen
   a. Isabella
   b. Josephine
   c. Elizabeth

121. Samuel Belkin, Norman Lamm, and Bernard Revel had one thing in common. They were all presidents of
   a. the same Orthodox seminary
   b. the same Reform seminary
   c. the same Conservative seminary

122. Louis Finkelstein, Bernard Revel, and Julian Morgenstern had one thing in common. They were all
   a. presidents of seminaries
   b. great Jewish philanthropists
   c. great Jewish athletes

123. Chaim Weizmann was the first president of the State of Israel. His nephew Ezer Weizman is a prominent Israeli. Ezer is famous for his

leadership as
  a. a scientist and inventor
  b. a general and a Minister of Defense
  c. a scholar and university president

124. Menachem Begin was Israel's Prime Minister in 1979 when the peace treaty with Egypt was signed. His immediate predecessors as Prime Minister were:
  a. Shimon Peres and Golda Meir
  b. Moshe Dayan and Yitzhak Rabin
  c. Golda Meir and Yitzhak Rabin

125. Three leaders of Judaism in the twentieth century were Solomon Schechter, Cyrus Adler, and Louis Finkelstein. All were presidents of
  a. an Orthodox seminary
  b. a Reform seminary
  c. a Conservative seminary

126. The early Zionist leader who more than any other influenced the life of Prime Minister Menachem Begin was
  a. Theodor Herzl
  b. Stephen S. Wise
  c. Vladimir Jabotinsky

127. The largest port in Israel is in
  a. Haifa
  b. Tel Aviv
  c. Ashdod

128. A person who emigrates to Israel and intends to settle there permanently is called
   a. an *oleh*
   b. a *shadchan*
   c. a *sabra*

129. Native-born Israelis are called *sabras*. The name was adopted from the name of the
   a. cactus plant
   b. city of Shechem, where the Samaritans live
   c. national bird of Israel

130. Anwar Sadat, president of Egypt, made peace with Israel in 1979. But he also started one of the wars against Israel. Which one?
   a. The Six-Day War
   b. The Yom Kippur War
   c. The War of Independence

131. The Egyptian leader who ruled Egypt before Anwar Sadat became president started the War of 1967 against Israel. His name is
   a. King Hussein
   b. Gamal Abdul Nasser.
   c. Yassir Arafat

132. One of the former presidents of the State of Israel was a scientist. His name is
   a. Yitzhak Navon

b. Moshe Sharett
c. Chaim Weizmann

133. *Ari* in Hebrew means "lion." A great scholar and mystic who lived in the 1500s was called "The Ari." His real name was
a. Moses Mendelssohn
b. Moses ben Maimon
c. Rabbi Isaac Luria

Language and
Literature

Part II – LANGUAGE AND LITERATURE

1. The American poet Emma Lazarus (1849-1887) wrote a poem entitled "The New Colossus." It gained great fame because it was inscribed on the

    a. Washington Monument
    b. Liberty Bell
    c. Statue of Liberty

2. A well-known author whose surname was Levin wrote *The Old Bunch, Compulsion, Eva*, and an autobiography, *In Search*. The full name of this author is

    a. Rachel Levin
    b. Shemaryahu Levin
    c. Meyer Levin

3. Many famous authors used Jews as leading characters in their writings: Shylock in Shakespeare's *The Merchant of Venice*, Barabas in Marlowe's *The Jew of Malta*, Fagin in Dickens' *Oliver Twist*, etc... Who was the leading character in Sir Walter Scott's *Ivanhoe?*

    a. Rachel
    b. Rebecca
    c. Riah

4. A classical, ethical work written in Hebrew in the 18th century is entitled *Mesillat Yesharim* (*The Way of the Righteous*). The author, a poet and kabbalist whose abbreviated name was *Ramchal*, was born in 1707 in Padua and died in 1747 in Palestine. His full name is

    a. Moses Mendelssohn
    b. Moses Maimonides
    c. Moses Chaim Luzzatto

5. *Fiddler on the Roof* was a successful Broadway play. The story in this play is based on the writings of

    a. William Shakespeare
    b. Sholom Aleichem
    c. Leonard Bernstein

6. The Book of Maccabees which describes the history of the Hasmonean family and the events that transpired in the days of Judah the

Maccabee (2nd century B.C.E.) is one of the books of the

   a. Mishna
   b. Apocrypha
   c. Bible

7. *Mah Tovu, Sim Shalom, Alenu* and *Sholom Aleichem* are the names of different

   a. Hebrew novels
   b. prayers
   c. Jewish authors

8. The anniversary of the death of a close relative is observed by kindling a light and reciting the Kaddish. It is called

   a. *yahrzeit*
   b. *matzevah*
   c. *yizkor*

9. A settlement in Israel, and sometimes the entire Jewish community, is referred to as the

   a. *knesset*
   b. *yeshiva*
   c. *yishuv*

10. A person who is a descendant of a family of distinction is said to have

    a. *yichus*
    b. *yahrzeit*
    c. *tashlich*

11. This American author, who was born in 1915 and is an Orthodox Jew, wrote *The Caine Mutiny, Marjorie Morningstar, Youngblood Hawke* and *This Is My God*. What is his name?

    a. Norman Mailer
    b. Maurice Samuel
    c. Herman Wouk

12. Which of the following words does *not* have any connection with the Talmud?

    a. *Yerushalmi*
    b. *Bavli*
    c. Essene

13. Leopold Zunz (1794-1886) was a noted German author who wrote many books on

    a. history, midrash and liturgy
    b. art and theater
    c. architecture and archaeology

14. Here are five expressions used by Jews in various parts of the world: 1) *mazzal u-vera-cha*, 2) *be-simman tov*, 3) *yeyasher koach*, 4) *chazak u-varuch*, 5) *tizkeh lemitzvot*. They all mean

    a. beware of evil
    b. until we meet again
    c. congratulations

15. Leon Uris, born in 1924, is an oustanding American novelist. He wrote *Battle Cry* (concerning World War II), and *Mila 18* (about the uprising in the Warsaw Ghetto). However, he is probably most famous for his novel about Israel entitled

    a. *Exodus*
    b. *The Source*
    c. *The Naked and the Dead*

16. *Forty Days of Musa Dagh* and *The Song of Bernadette* were outstanding novels written by this Jewish poet and playwright, born in Prague in 1890. He died in the U.S. in 1945, having moved here in 1940. His name is

    a. Samuel Goldwyn
    b. Franz Werfel
    c. Sholem Asch

17. A popular book by the French novelist André Schwarz-Bart is based upon the talmudic statement that the world is kept in existence through the merits of 36 *tzaddikim* (righteous men) in each generation. What is the name of that book?

    a. *Judgment in Nuremberg*
    b. *Judgment and Destiny*
    c. *The Last of the Just*

18. The Hebrew phrase meaning "merit of the fathers" refers to the pious deeds of Abraham, Isaac and Jacob. The exact Hebrew phrase is

    a. *pidyon haben*
    b. *zechus avos*
    c. *shalom zachor*

19. The hymn found in the prayerbook known as *Yigdal* was composed in Italy in the 13th century. It is based upon the "Thirteen Principles of Faith" outlined a century earlier by a famous Jewish philosopher. His name is

    a. Moses Maimonides
    b. Moses ben Nachman
    c. Moses of Coucy

20. The Hebrew expression which is sometimes used when speaking of a deceased person, and meaning "of blessed memory," is

   a. *zichrono livrocho*
   b. *l'chayim*
   c. *l'hitraot*

21. Emile Hertzog, born in 1885, is a well-known French author. He achieved fame when his book *Les Silences de Colonel Bramble* appeared. He also wrote biographies of Shelley and Disraeli, and histories of France, England and the U.S. His autobiography is entitled *Call No Man Happy*. He is best known by his pen-name which is

   a. André Maurois
   b. Leon Blum
   c. Emile Zola

22. This man was born in Russia in 1887. He came to the U.S. in 1903 and taught Jewish literature and philosophy at Harvard from 1915 to 1958. He was promoted to professor in 1925. Among his important works are *Philo* and *The Philosophy of Spinoza*. What is his name?

   a. Louis Ginzberg
   b. Harry Austryn Wolfson
   c. Abraham Joshua Heschel

23. Boris Pasternak was a baptized Jew who was born in 1890 and died in 1960. He was awarded the Nobel Prize in Literature in 1958, after the publication of one of his books, but refused to accept it. The name of the book is

    a. *Crime and Punishment*
    b. *Dr. Zhivago*
    c. *The Naked and the Dead*

24. The Hebrew phrase for "holiday" which has the literal meaning of "good day" is

    a. *yom ha-din*
    b. *yom tov*
    c. *yom teruah*

25. The dagger-like strokes that look like crowns and appear on some of the letters in hand-written copies of the Torah are called

    a. *tagin*
    b. *massorah*
    c. *trop*

26. Marie Syrkin wrote *Blessed Is the Match*, based on a poem by the same name. The author of the poem was a courageous woman who parachuted into Yugoslavia in 1944 in order to rescue prisoners and organize Jewish resistance to

the Nazis. She was captured and shot in Budapest after standing trial. Her name is

   a. Anne Frank
   b. Hanna Szenes
   c. Mathilda Schechter

27. A Professor of Jewish History at Yeshiva University until his death in 1955, this scholar was born in 1882. He did a great deal of work for the Hebrew Immigrant Aid Society (HIAS) and wrote a book about their activities entitled *Visas to Freedom*. Ten years after his death his most important work appeared entitled, *A History of Jewish Crafts and Guilds*, which was seen through the press by his wife, Rachel. What was this scholar's name?

   a. Mark W. Wischnitzer
   b. Salo W. Baron
   c. Harry A. Wolfson

28. Menahem Ribalow (1895-1953) was the editor of a weekly Hebrew magazine from 1922 (one year after his arrival in America), until his death in 1953. The name of the periodical is

   a. *Bitzaron*
   b. *Hatzofeh*
   c. *Hadoar*

29. The sacrifice of the red heifer is described in the Bible in the Book of Numbers. Its ashes, when mixed with water, were used to purify an unclean person who had come in contact with the dead. The Hebrew name for the red heifer is

    a. *aygel hazahov*
    b. *parah adumah*
    c. *chad gadya*

30. This Rumanian-born writer (1895) came to the United States in 1914, and was the author of such popular works as *Harvest in the Desert, The Great Hatred,* and *The Gentlemen and the Jews.* His name is

    a. Maurice Samuel
    b. Herman Wouk
    c. Yigal Yadin

31. The eternal lamp that burns continuously in every synagogue, and is first mentioned in the Bible in the Book of Leviticus (chapter 6, verse 6), is called in Hebrew

    a. *havdalah* candle
    b. *yahrzeit* lamp
    c. *ner tamid*

32. Jewish legend speaks of a river that flows all week long, but rests completely on the Sabbath day. The name of the river is

   a. Euphrates
   b. Sambatyon
   c. Tigris

33. The term for a native Israeli is the same as the Arabic word meaning a "prickly pear" cactus. The term was adopted because this type of cactus, which is supposed to characterize the native Israeli, has a tough exterior and a tender interior. The Arabic word is

   a. *Yisraeli*
   a. *sabra*
   c. *Yehudi*

34. The Hebrew term for the sacrifice of Isaac actually means "the binding." It is called the

   a. *akeda*
   b. *moloch*
   c. *mincha*

35. The book entitled *Beliefs and Opinions* was written in Arabic by Saadya ben Joseph, who was also known as Saadya Gaon. Saadya was born in Egypt in 882, but spent much time in Palestine and Babylonia. This important work

of Saadya, which denies any conflict between
reason and revealed religion, was translated
into Hebrew by Judah Ibn Tibbon in 1186. The
Hebrew title of the book is

   a. *Moreh Nevuchim*
   b. *Machzor Vitri*
   c. *Emunot VeDeot*

36. Judah Loeb Pinsker was an outstanding
pioneer of the Zionist movement. In 1882, he
published a pamphlet, that has become famous,
which proclaimed that Jews could save themselves from anti-Semitism by the establishment
of a Jewish state. The name of the pamphlet is

   a. *Der Judenstadt*
   b. *Birobidjan*
   c. *Auto-Emancipation*

37. An important Yiddish writer who was
born in Russia in 1852 is still remembered for
his stirring stories, many of which have been
translated into English. Perhaps his most famous story is "Bontsche Schweig," written in
1888. His first and middle names are Isaac Leib.
His last name is

   a. Asch
   b. Singer
   c. Peretz

38. A Yiddish author of Polish birth (1886) settled in the U.S. in 1907. He wrote hundreds of stories and novels, some of which were translated into English and other languages. Some of the better known of his works are *In Polish Fields*, describing Hassidic life in the mid-19th century, and *The Last Revolt* dealing with the Bar Kochba period. The name of the author, who died in 1954, is

    a. Norman Mailer
    b. Joseph Opatoshu
    c. Sholem Asch

39. One of the great Jewish figures of the 18th century was born in Dessau, Germany, in 1729. He studied in Berlin where he became proficient in philosophy, mathematics, Latin, French and English. He translated a good many of the books of the Bible into German, and devoted much of his time to writing books and treatises in defense of Jewish rights. The hero in *Nathan the Wise* is modeled after this leading Jewish figure. His name is

    a. Moses Mendelssohn
    b. Simon Dubnow
    c. Heinrich Graetz

40. Alexander Marx (1878-1954) came to the United States from Germany as a young man to join the faculty of the Jewish Theological Seminary of America. He wrote a book, together with Max Margolis, entitled

    a. *History of the Jewish People*
    b. *The Communist Manifesto*
    c. *Conservative Judaism*

41. A Jewish author who was born in 1880, in Poland, and who died in 1957, in Israel, wrote books in Yiddish that were translated into English. Among them were *The Nazarene, The Apostle,* and *Mary.* He was widely criticized in many Jewish circles. What was his name?

    a. Chaim Nachman Bialik
    b. Shaul Tschernichovsky
    c. Sholem Asch

42. Shalom Jacob Abramowitsch was the pen-name of a famous Hebrew and Yiddish author. He was born in Russia in 1836 and died in 1917. Among his famous books are *Fishke the Lame, The Meat Tax* and the autobiographical novel *In Those Days.* His pen-name was

    a. Sholom Aleichem
    b. I. L. Peretz
    c. Mendele Mocher Sephorim

43. Although the Hebrew phrase *am ha-aretz*, literally means "people of the land," the actual, colloquial meaning is

a. farmer
b. ignoramus
c. Zionist

44. A famous English author, born of poor Russian parents in London, began to make his fame while teaching at the Jews' Free School. He was born in 1864 and died in 1926. Among his better known books are *Children of the Ghetto* and *The King of the Schnorrers.* His name is

a. Judah Touro
b. Benjamin Disraeli
c. Israel Zangwill

45. Sholom Aleichem was called "the Mark Twain of Yiddish literature." He was born in 1859, and died in 1916. He wrote poems, novels and dramas in Yiddish, Hebrew and Russian. The Broadway play *Fiddler on the Roof* is based on one of his stories. Sholom was a pen-name. His real name was

a. Zalman Shneour
b. Sholom Spiegel
c. Shalom Rabinovich

46. This great English scholar was born in 1858 and died in 1925. In 1888, together with Claude Montefiore he founded the *Jewish Quarterly Review*. He served on the faculty of Jews' College from 1891 to 1902 and also taught at Cambridge. His name was Israel Abrahams. Which of these well-known books did he write?

    a. *A Guide for the Perplexed*
    b. *The Apocrypha*
    c. *Jewish Life in the Middle Ages*

47. Abbreviations are very common in Hebrew, as in all languages. Which of these is the Hebrew abbreviation for Bible, and what are the three words for which the abbreviation stands?

    a. Rashi
    b. Tanach
    c. Rambam

48. The accents or musical notes that guide the person reading the Torah are called

    a. *chazeres* or *karpas*
    b. *sidra* or *parsha*
    c. *neginot* or *te'amim*

49. S. Y. Agnon (Shmuayl Yosayf Agnon) was born in Galicia in 1888. One of his famous books was called

    a. *The Mishne Torah*

    b. *The Bridal Canopy*

    c. *Tale of Two Cities*

50. This English poet and novelist was born in 1816 and died in 1847. She was of Marrano ancestry. Her most popular book was a romantic novel about the Marrano (secret) Jews of Spain entitled *Vale of Cedars*. Her name is

    a. Grace Aguilar

    b. Kathleen Windsor

    c. Yael Yadin

51. Asher Ginsberg was a famous essayist and philosopher. He was born in the Ukraine in 1856 and died in Palestine in 1927, after having settled there in 1922. Among his well-known books are *Al Parashat Derachim* (*At the Crossroads*) and *Al Shete Ha-Se'ipim* (*Wavering Between Two Opinions*). He was opposed to Herzl's idea of a Jewish *political* state in Palestine favoring, rather, a *spiritual* center in Palestine. His pen-name was

    a. Rambam

    b. Ahad Ha'am

    c. Sholom Aleichem

52. The English alphabet has 26 letters in it. How many are in the Hebrew alphabet?

    a. 22, which includes 5 final letters
    b. 22, and no final letters
    c. 22, plus 5 final letters

53. The Hebrew word meaning "to go up" or "ascend" is used to describe the honor bestowed upon a person called to recite the blessings over the Torah. The word is

    a. *aliyah*
    b. *berachah*
    c. *kaddish*

54. The Spanish *Auto-de-Fé*, which began towards the end of the 15th century, was a sad chapter in Jewish history. At a public ceremony, sentences of the Inquisition were announced to the victims. This was followed by a public burning outside the city limits (where so-called heretics were burned). What does *Auto-de-Fé* mean?

    a. Save the King
    b. Praise the Church
    c. Act of Faith

55. The opposite of a *mitzvah* is

   a. an *averah*
   b. an *esrog*
   c. a *minyan*

56. A Jewish historian who has been professor of Jewish history, literature and institutions at Columbia University since 1930 wrote the following important works: *A Social and Religious History of the Jews, Modern Nationalism and Religion,* and *The Jewish Community.* What is his name?

   a. Louis Finkelstein
   b. Salo W. Baron
   c. Harry Wolfson

57. Saul Bellow is a novelist who was born in Canada in 1915 and who has taught at various American universities. His most famous novel is

   a. *Gone With the Wind*
   b. *The Caine Mutiny*
   c. *The Adventures of Augie March*

58. Eliezer Ben Yehudah was born in Lithuania in 1858. When he came to Palestine in 1881,

he changed his name from Perelmann to Ben Yehudah. He is most famous for

   a. writing a comprehensive dictionary of ancient and modern Hebrew
   b. the part he played as a warrior in the War of Liberation
   c. teaching young actors and singers

59. *The Wisdom of Ben Sira* was written by a Jewish sage who lived in Jerusalem in the 2nd century B.C.E. This book, also known as *Ecclesiasticus*, was translated into the Greek by Ben Sira's son in 132 B.C.E., and was incorporated in the *Apocrypha*. The book contains

   a. wise proverbs and sayings
   b. wise advice about medical matters
   c. new ideas about the prophets

60. Benjamin of Tudela lived in Spain in the 12th century. He is best known for a book he wrote which was not published until 1543. The subject matter of the book is

   a. his travels to 300 different places
   b. his ideas on astrology and astronomy
   c. his interpretation of the Bible and Talmud

61. Chaim Nachman Bialik was a famous poet who was born in Russia in 1873 and moved to Israel in 1924. One of his most famous poems is about the yeshiva student. It is called

    a. Hamasmid
    b. Ir Ha-harega
    c. Megillas Ha-esh

62. A Hebrew monthly devoted to philosophy, literature, and current events was established in 1939 by Chaim Tchernowitz, a noted scholar who edited the magazine until his death in 1949. The magazine is called

    a. *Commentary*
    b. *Hadoar*
    c. *Bitzaron*

63. B'nai B'rith is a Jewish service organization founded in 1843 with lodges all over the world. What do the Hebrew words *b'nai b'rith* mean?

    a. children of Israel
    b. sons of the covenant
    c. members of the tribe

64. Léon Blum started his career as a literary critic and author, and then became involved in the socialist movement in France. The high

point of his career was reached in 1936 when he
became

    a. Premier of France in the Popular Front
        Government
    b. a Nobel prize winner for his literary
        achievements
    c. Chairman of the Board of the Jewish
        Agency

65. *For the Sake of Heaven, I and Thou,* and
Tales of the Hasidism are important published
works. Their author is

    a. The Lubavitcher Rebbe
    b. Gedalia Bublick
    c. Martin Buber

66. Abraham Cahan, a Yiddish journalist
and editor, was born in Lithuania in 1860 and
came to America in 1882. He was the editor of
the Yiddish newspaper *Forverts* (or *Forwards*)
for about 50 years. He wrote an English novel
entitled

    a. *King of the Schnorers*
    b. *The Jewish Caravan*
    c. *The Rise of David Levinsky*

67. One of the names of the twelve Hebrew months means father. Which is it?

 a. Elul
 b. Av
 c. Adar

68. The following three Hebrew phrases all mean the same thing: *bet ha-kevarot, bet olam,* and *bet hayyim.* They all mean

 a. synagogue
 b. cemetery
 c. house of study

69. *Nachas* is a Yiddish expression that has its original in the Hebrew language. It means

 a. pain and privation
 b. poverty and sickness
 c. peace, pleasure, or contentment

70. Helm (also spelled Chelm) is a Polish town whose Jewish settlement dates back to the 15th century. The Jewish residents figure in many anecdotes in which their main characteristic is their

 a. wisdom
 b. kindness
 c. naiveté

71. George Clemenceau, a great French statesman (1841-1929) was a leading defender of a Jewish French army captain accused of betraying France. Clemenceau edited the newspaper in which Émil Zola's famous book, *J'accuse* first appeared. What was the name of the Jewish captain who was falsely accused?

    a. Léon Blum
    b. Alfred Dreyfus
    c. Moses Hess

72. The *shekel,* the *peruta* and the *agora* have been used in both ancient and modern Israel. These are

    a. measures of weight
    b. types of coins
    c. types of food

73. There are many ways of saying "congratulations" in Hebrew. Which one of the following is *not* a congratulatory phrase?

    a. *yeyasher koach*
    b. *mazal tov*
    c. *yaale v'yavo*

74. The confession of sins is a prominent feature of Jewish liturgy, particularly on the Day

of Atonement. The best known example is the
Al Het, which is an enumeration of various
types of sins. The Hebrew term for confession
of sins is

    a. *kiddush*
    b. *viddui*
    c. *kaddish*

75. The Hebrew word for charity is *tzedakah,*
but the literal meaning of the Hebrew word is

    a. pity
    b. righteousness
    c. comfort

76. An Austrian author who was born in
1881 and died in 1942 wrote the pacifist drama,
Jeremiah, as well as several successful biographies including *Marie Antoinette, Mary, Queen
of Scots,* and *Joseph Fouché.* He lived in England
for a while and then sought refuge from the
Nazis in Brazil where he committed suicide. His
autobiography, *The World of Yesterday,* was
published after his death. His name is

    a. Alfred Dreyfus
    b. Leopold Zung
    c. Stefan Zweig

77. A personality in the talmudic literature of the first century C.E. has much in common with the Rip Van Winkle of American literature who slept for twenty years. The talmudic character slept for 70 years. He was also famous for drawing a circle around himself, then praying for rain, and not leaving the circle until his prayers were answered. This person's name is

    a. Elisha ben Avuyah
    b. Honi Ha-meaggel
    c. Akiba ben Joseph

78. The Arabic word *ibn* and the Aramaic word *bar*, both meaning "son," have the same meaning as the Hebrew word

    a. *baal*
    b. *bas*
    c. *ben*

79. The following three Hebrew words and phrases have the same meaning: *yamim tovim*, *haggim*, and *moadim*. They all refer to

    a. holidays
    b. fast days
    c. birth days

80. A Hebrew phrase meaning "profanation of the Name (of God)," refers to any action by

a Jew that would bring disgrace upon Jews or Judaism. The actual Hebrew phrase is

a. *kiddush ha-Shem*
b. *hillul ha-Shem*
b. *sholom aleichem*

81. The leader of the service who chants the prayers in the synagogue is called a

a. *baal koray*
b. *hazzan*
c. *bais k'nesses*

82. Although automation is a recent innovation, the idea of an automaton in human form, created by magical means, dates back to talmudic days. Stories of such a creature recur in Jewish literature up to the 16th century, and the most famous is associated with Rabbi Judah Low ben Bezalel of Prague (the Maharal). What is this automaton called in Hebrew?

a. *golem*
b. *galus*
c. *gedula*

83. Since the name of God in Hebrew was treated with special sanctity, in writing two

different Hebrew letters, in particular, are used instead of the actual name. These letters are

    a. *alef and bet*
    b. *daled and hay*
    c. *yad and alef*

84. One of the most remarkable works by a single individual in all Jewish literature was an eleven volume history of the Jews written by a German Bible scholar and historian who was born in 1817 and died in 1891. It was written in German and was later translated into a six volume English edition. The set is entitled *History of the Jews*. The author is

    a. Theodore Herzl
    b. Ismar Elbogen
    c. Heinrich Graetz

85. One of the popular sections of the Passover *Haggadah* which has the same style as the poem "The House That Jack Built" was composed in the 15th century. The name of this selection is

    a. *Adon Olam*
    b. *Chad Gadya*
    c. *Ma Nishtana*

86. The Israel airline, established in 1949, now carries passengers and freight to four continents. It was named El Al. These two Hebrew words mean

    a. all for one
    b. for everybody
    c. on high

87. Naphtali Herz Imber (1856-1909) was a Hebrew poet who, during his lifetime, lived in Galicia, Rumania, Turkey and Palestine. His most famous poem is

    a. *Adon Olam*
    b. *Hatikvah*
    c. *Yigdal*

88. The three Hebrew words or phrases *kol nidre*, *al chet*, and *ashamnu* refer to prayers that are recited during

    a. the circumcision ceremony
    b. the Torah reading
    c. the Yom Kippur service

89. The Protocols of the Elders of Zion is a famous book first published in Russia in 1903. This book has been in print for all these many years, and is considered to be

    a. the platform of the first Zionist convention

    b. the main source for information about the Second Temple

    c. the Bible of the anti-Semites

90. Four well-known novels about contemporary Jewish life are *The Chosen, The Promise, Exodus,* and *Herzog.* Most of them were written by

    a. Saul Bellow

    b. Chaim Potok

    c. Leon Uris

91. In 1882, a doctor named Leon Pinsker wrote *Auto-Emancipation,* a book in which he said Jews will free themselves of discrimination only when

    a. they have a land of their own

    b. they convert to the religion of the majority

    c. they all learn to speak German perfectly

92. In 1966, S.Y. Agnon, an Israeli, won the Nobel Prize for Literature. In 1978 a second Jewish writer was awarded the Nobel Prize. His name is

    a. Isaac Bashevis Singer

    b. Chaim Nachman Bialik

    c. Isaac Babel

93. The Yiddish language is made up of several languages. Although it consists of many Hebrew words, most of the words come from the
   a. French language.
   b. German language.
   c. Russian language.

94. The Western Wall that still stands in Jerusalem was once part of the Temple compound. We also call it the Wailing Wall. Its original Hebrew name is
   a. *Yerushalayim.*
   b. *Yad Vashem.*
   c. *Kotel Maaravi.*

95. Western Jews customarily use the *ashkenazic* Hebrew pronunciation. Eastern Jews and Israelis use the
   a. biblical pronunciation.
   b. talmudic pronunciation.
   c. sephardic pronunciation.

Institutions

Part III – INSTITUTIONS

1. The Israeli organization known as *Magen David Adom* is the equivalent of the international organization known as the

 a. Red Cross
 b. Blue Shield
 c. Blue Cross

2. Maidanek, Terezin and Treblinka are remembered in Jewish history because they were

 a. centers of Jewish Learning
 b. the native cities of three great prophets
 c. Nazi extermination camps

3. The first president of the Hebrew University was a Reform rabbi in New York City in his younger years. He was born in 1877 and died in 1948. His name is

 a. Abba Hillel Silver
 b. Mordecai Manuel Noah
 c. Judah Leon Magnes

4. A well-known organization in Israel is called Mapai. The name Mapai is made up of the initials of the Hebrew words, *mifleget poale eretz yisrael*, which means

    a. Israel map-makers' organization
    b. Israel manufacturers' organization
    c. Israel workers' party

5. In Israel, an institute for the intensive study of Hebrew for new immigrants is known as the

    a. *ulpan*
    b. *kibbutz*
    c. *moshava*

6. The organization responsible for the transfer of young persons to Israel and educating them there was initiated by Recha Freyer in the early 1930's because of German anti-Semitism. From 1933-45, it was headed by Henrietta Szold. It was called

    a. Youth Aliyah
    b. *Kibbutzim*
    c. *Eretz Yisrael*

7. The United Jewish Appeal was organized in 1939 to coordinate the fund-raising campaigns of three organizations: 1) the United

Palestine Appeal, 2) the American Joint Distribution Committee, and 3) the

   a. Zionist Organization of America
   b. American Jewish Congress
   c. National Refugee Service

8. The United Synagogue of America is an organization of synagogues closely related to the

   a. Jewish Theological Seminary
   b. Hebrew Union College
   c. Yeshiva University

9. Two Temples were built in Jerusalem. The first was built by King Solomon, and was destroyed in the year 586 B.C.E., by Nebuchadnezzer of Babylonia. The second Temple was destroyed

   a. in the year 333 B.C.E. by the Persians
   b. in the year 70 B.C.E. by the Greeks
   c. in the year 70 C.E. by the Romans

10. One Jewish organization, recognized by the U.S. government, works very closely with the soldiers and sailors in the military service.

Which one is it, and what do the initials stand
for?

    a. J.N.F.
    b. U.J.A.
    c. J.W.B.

11. For many years, one of these institutions
has helped hundreds of immigrants who have
come to America from countries in all parts of
the world. Which one is it, and what do the
initials stand for?

    a. J.T.S.
    b. H.I.A.S.
    c. U.A.H.C.

12. *Yad Va-shem*, meaning "monument and
name," is an organization established in Israel
in 1953 to

    a. commemorate the establishment of the
       State of Israel
    b. honor Jewish recipients of the Nobel
       Prize
    c. commemorate the massacre of Jews in
       Nazi era

13. A fraternal insurance society was created
by Jewish immigrant workers in 1900. In 1933,
it helped to create the Jewish Labor Committee.

Its Yiddish name is *Arbeiter Ring*. What is its English name?

    a. American Jewish Committee
    b. Hebrew Immigrants Aid Society
    c. Workmen's Circle

14. The National Federation of Temple Sisterhoods and the National Association of Temple Educators are related to which of these organizations?

    a. United Synagogue of America
    b. Union of Orthodox Jewish Congregations
    c. Union of American Hebrew Congregations

15. The Institute for Jewish Research, which was founded in Vilna in 1925, and by 1939 had branches in 30 countries, is called

    a. YIVO (Yidisher Visenshaftlicher Institut)
    b. WIZO
    c. HIAS

16. This woman, who never married, was born in Baltimore in 1860 where her father was

a rabbi for 40 years. She was secretary of the Jewish Publication Society of America from 1892-1919. In 1912, she organized Hadassah, the Women's Zionist Organization of America. Her name is

    a. Golda Meir
    b. Henrietta Szold
    c. Frances Perkins

17. One of the most influential American Jews of his time, he established, and was the rabbi of the Free Synagogue in New York City (1907); he was the founder of the American Jewish Congress (1925); he was a founder of the Federation of American Zionists (which later became the Zionist Organization of America); and he founded the Jewish Institute of Religion (1922). He was born in 1874 and died in 1949. What is his name?

    a. Stephen S. Wise
    b. Judah Magnes
    c. Abba Hillel Silver

18. A Zionist organization was organized in London in 1920 and has done much to help Jewish children, in particular, settle in Palestine. It

has branches in 53 countries but none in America. What is its name?

    a. WIZO (Women's International Zionist Organization)
    b. World Jewish Congress
    c. Hadassah

19. This rabbi was born in 1819 in Bohemia and died in 1900. He is called the "Father of Reform Judaism in the U.S." He was the first president of the Hebrew Union College, organized in 1875 in Cincinnati, Ohio. His name is

    a. Isaac Mayer Wise
    b. Stephen S. Wise
    c. Jonah B. Wise

20. A school of thought which contends that Judaism is not only a religion, but a civilization, was initiated by Rabbi Mordecai M. Kaplan in 1934. It had a profound effect on many Conservative and Reform Jews, and is called

    a. Reconstructionism
    b. Liberalism
    c. Neo-Orthodoxy

21. The Samaritans were a Hebrew sect that had its beginnings in biblical days and still survives, although very few members are left. They

were not part of the stream of Judaism as it developed through the centuries because

    a. they did not believe in Moses
    b. they did not accept the Talmud
    c. they refused to observe Passover

22. An important Jewish sect during the period of the second Temple was the Sadducees. They believed in a literal translation of the Bible. The major group that opposed them was called the

    a. Nazarenes
    b. Nazirites
    c. Pharisees

23. There are three major Jewish religious denominations: Orthodox, Conservative and Reform. The Reform group also calls itself

    a. Neo-orthodox
    b. Liberal
    c. Reconstructionist

24. The following six men had one particular thing in common: Stephen S. Wise, Isaac Mayer

Wise, Kaufmann Kohler, Sabato Morais, Bernard Revel and Cyrus Adler. They were all

    a. rabbis
    b. presidents of theological seminaries
    c. presidents of the Zionist Organization of America

25. Three major seminaries have been on the American scene for more than 75 years. The Hebrew Union College was organized in 1875 and merged in 1950 with the Jewish Institute of Religion. The Jewish Theological Seminary was organized in 1886, and the Rabbi Isaac Elchanan Theological Seminary was organized in 1896. Which of the three is part of Yeshiva University?

    a. Hebrew Union College
    b. Jewish Theological Seminary
    c. Rabbi Isaac Elchanan Theological Seminary

26. Max Nordau was born in Budapest in 1849 and died in 1923. He practiced medicine and also pursued a careed in journalism. However, he is best known for his efforts on behalf of

    a. the Zionist movement
    b. medical research
    c. the plight of the workingman

27. An organization was founded in Germany in 1864 which called itself *Mekitze Nirdamim*, meaning "rousers of the slumbering." In 1934 it moved its headquarters to Jerusalem. The purpose of the organization was to

    a. help poor Jews who were wasting their years

    b. support hospitals with incurable patients

    c. print old Hebrew writings never before published

28. In 1917 this organization was founded to protect the rights of Jews. Its most famous president was Rabbi Stephen S. Wise. What is the name of this organization?

    a. American Jewish Congress

    b. United Jewish Appeal

    c. American Jewish Committee

29. An organization was founded in 1906 "to prevent the infraction of civil and religious rights of Jews in any part of the world." Its past presidents have included Mayer Sulzberger, Louis Marshall, Cyrus Adler, and Joseph M. Proskauer. It publishes a magazine called *Commentary*. What is the name of the organization?

    a. American Jewish Congress

    b. United Jewish Appeal

    c. American Jewish Committee

30. Bar-Ilan is a famous institution in Israel named after Rabbi Meir Berlin (who changed his name to Bar-Ilan). The purpose of the institution, which was founded in 1955, is to

    a. educate young people
    b. heal sick people
    c. help find homes for orphans

31. The basic program of Zionism was adopted at the First Zionist Congress in 1897. It is known by the name of the city where it was promulgated. The program is called

    a. the Basle Program
    b. the Cincinnati Program
    c. the Geneva Program

32. A scholar and educator, born in Poland in 1911 became the president of Yeshiva University in 1943. His name is

    a. Bernard Revel
    b. Samuel Belkin
    c. Pincus Churgin

33. *B'nei Akiva* is a Zionist youth movement, organized in 1929. Its purpose is to train young

people to settle and study in Israel. It is affiliated with

 a. *Histadrut Ivrit*
 b. *Hapoel Hamizrachi*
 c. the Zionist Organization of America

34. The term *Bais Din* is most closely related
to which of the following?

 a. *Bais Knesset*
 b. *Sanhedrin*
 c. *Beth Hamidrash*

35. Bezalel is a famous school in Israel
founded in 1906 by Boris Schatz. The main purpose of the school is to teach

 a. geography and history
 b. oceanography and archaeology
 c. arts and crafts

36. A *Chevra Kadisha* is a society whose func-
tion is to

 a. care for all the details of a wedding
 b. care for all the details of a *pidyon haben*
 c. care for all the details of burial

37. There were many controversies in Jewish
history between individuals, schools of thought,
and groups. One example of such conflict was

between Hillel and Shammai. Which of the following groups were not in direct, face to face conflict?

    a. Samaritans and Reconstructionists
    b. Chasidim and Misnagdim
    c. Pharisees and Sadducees

38. In 1924 the Chicago Board of Jewish Education organized a school of higher Jewish learning in which teachers might be trained. It was called

    a. Yeshiva University
    b. Hebrew Union College
    c. College of Jewish Studies

39. Morris Raphael Cohen (1880-1947) was an outstanding teacher and philosopher. His books on the logic of the natural and social sciences include *Reason and Nature*, and *Law and the Social Order*. From 1938-42 he taught at the University of Chicago, but he is best known for his years of teaching at another school from 1912-38. The name of the school is

    a. Yeshiva University
    b. The City College of New York
    c. New York University

40. Nathan Krochmal, Zacharias Frankel, Heinrich Graetz, Isaac Leeser and Sabato Morais were 19th century scholars whose points of view were in keeping with the ideas developed by which branch of Judaism?

    a. Orthodox Judaism
    b. Reform Judaism
    c. Conservative Judaism

41. The *Baal Shem Tov* is a name associated with a great religious and social movement in Judaism. The founder of the movement was Israel Baal Shem Tov (1699-1761). His whole life was spent in Volhynia and Podolia, but his influence spread throughout Europe and subsequently to America. The movement is called

    a. *Haskalah*
    b. *Halutzim*
    c. *Hasidism*

42. The flag of Israel has a Star of David in the center and two broad stripes on either side of the star. The rest of the flag can be described as

    a. white with blue stripes
    b. blue with white stripes
    c. white with black stripes

43. A secret organization was established in Palestine to protect the Jewish population during the rule of the British. It was created in 1920 and was discontinued in 1948 (becoming a part of the regular army), when Israel became a nation. The name of the group was

   a. *Haganah*
   b. *Hadassah*
   c. *Habima*

44. The women's Zionist Organization of America has over 300,000 members spread over every state of the United States. It was founded in 1912 by Henrietta Szold. The name of the organization is

   a. *Habonim*
   b. *Haganah*
   c. *Hadassah*

45. One of the first Zionist pioneering movements was founded in Kharkov, Russia, in 1882. It had as its motto the initials of the Hebrew words for the verse in Isaiah (Chapter 2, verse 5), "O house of Jacob, come ye, and let us go." What was the name of this organization?

   a. BILU
   b. YIVO
   c. HIAS

46. Sura and Pumbedita were famous because they were

    a. the seat of great academies of learning
    b. the first to print a Hebrew book
    c. great comedians in the Middle Ages

47. Menahem Begin was born in Poland in 1913. In 1942, he arrived in Palestine and became the commander of an underground organization of fighters that battled the British. The organization was called

    a. *Irgun*
    b. *Kibbutz*
    c. *Neture Karta*

48. The name of the group which was sent by England to Palestine, in 1936, to study the political situation, and which finally recommended the partition of Palestine into two sovereign and independent states (one Arab and one Jewish) was called the

    a. Peel Commission
    b. Balfour Commission
    c. United Nations Commission

49. Israel has many universities. Only one of Israel's larger cities has two major universities. That city is

a. Jerusalem
b. Haifa
c. Tel Aviv

Bible

Part IV – BIBLE

1. When the sons of Jacob came to Egypt to buy food, they were accused by Joseph of being men of bad character. What, specifically, were they accused of?

    a. of being thieves
    b. of being spies
    c. of being kidnappers

2. Jacob wrestled with a man all night long and defeated him. As a result Jacob was given a new name. His new name was

    a. Aaron
    b. Noah
    c. Israel

3. Abraham had a nephew whose name was Lot. Lot's wife is famous because she looked backwards, and, as a result, turned into a pillar of salt. What did she see when she looked backwards?

    a. She saw Jacob's ladder reaching to the heavens
    b. She saw Cain kill Abel and refused to tell
    c. She saw the wicked city of Sodom being destroyed

4. Before the flood came, Noah built an ark.
He lived in it for 150 days until the flood was
over. Before he came out he sent two birds, at
different times, to see if it was safe to leave the
ark. Which birds did he send?

    a. a raven and a robin
    b. a swallow and a raven
    c. a raven and a dove

5. Wars were very common in Bible days.
Some interesting laws are laid down in the Book
of Deuteronomy on how to act in wartime.
Which one of these is *not* mentioned in the Bible?

    a. All fruit trees may not be cut down in
       wartime
    b. No men may be taken prisoners in war-
       time
    c. A soldier who is afraid should be sent
       home

6. Abraham sent his servant to find a wife
for his son. The servant met a young girl near
a well, drawing some water. "May I have some
water?" he asked. She gave him some water and
said: "I will draw water for your camels, too!"
Who was the servant and who was the girl?

    a. Isaac and Rebekah
    b. Jacob and Leah
    c. Eliezer and Rebekah

7. Three women who were related to Moses, played an important part in his life. Which set of women was related to Moses?

   a. Zipporah, Jochebed, Miriam
   b. Miriam, Jochebed, Dinah
   c. Jochebed, Rachel, Miriam

8. In chapter 11 of Leviticus, certain types of animals are described as kosher (fit to eat), and certain ones are described as not being kosher. The main characteristic of a kosher animal is that it

   a. has split hooves and smooth skin
   b. chews the cud and has split hooves
   c. chews the cud and lives on a farm

9. Joseph was a dreamer. His brothers hated him because in his dreams he was more important than they. Which of the following did Joseph dream?

   a. that the sun, moon and stars bowed down to him
   b. that a ladder reached to heaven and Joseph was on top of it
   c. that a rainbow in the sky appeared at Joseph's command

10. While in the desert, the children of Israel complained that they were hungry. God sent food in the form of dew which lay on the ground each morning. It tasted like wafers made with honey. What did the Israelites call it?

    a. They called it *lechem*
    b. They called it *geffen*
    c. They called it *manna*

11. After Joseph told his brothers who he really was, he sent them back home to bring their father Jacob, and their families, down to Egypt. Joseph set aside one city in Egypt for his family to live in. What was the name of that city?

    a. Canaan
    b. Goshen
    c. Shechem

12. Which sets of women listed below were not married to either Abraham, Isaac or Jacob?

    a. Dinah and Zipporah
    b. Hagar and Rachel
    c. Eve and Ruth

13. During the years of famine, Jacob and his family lived in Canaan. Joseph was in Egypt at the time. Jacob sent his sons to Egypt to buy food. Who recognized whom when the brothers

came to Egypt and faced Joseph for the first time?

   a. Joseph recognized his brothers first
   b. The brothers recognized Joseph first
   c. Only Joseph and Benjamin recognized each other

14. Isaac and his wife Rebekah had two sons. They were twins. What were their names?

   a. Shem and Japhet
   b. Cain and Abel
   c. Jacob and Esau

15. Three men played an important part in the life of Moses. They were all related to him. Who were they?

   a. Jethro, Amram and Joseph
   b. Aaron, Amram and Ephraim
   c. Aaron, Jethro and Amram

16. In chapter 31, the Book of Proverbs has some very complimentary things to say about the woman who is a good wife and a good mother. Which of these expressions did it use?

   a. Woman of Valour
   b. Woman of Honor
   c. Woman of Courage

17. "Four score and seven years ago . . ." is the way Lincoln's Gettysburg Address begins. One of the books in the Bible uses a figure of speech very similar to it. It reads "The length of our life is seventy years, or by reason of strength, four score years. . . ." In which book of the Bible is this found?

    a. the Book of Genesis
    b. the Book of Isaiah
    c. the Book of Psalms

18. The Latin translation of the Bible was written in Palestine between the years 390-405, by Church Father Jerome. The translation, which became the official version of the Catholic Church, is known as the

    a. Vulgate
    b. Apocrypha
    c. Zohar

19. Of the twelve tribes among whom Palestine was divided when the children of Israel entered Canaan after the death of Moses, two were not the names of Jacob's twelve sons. Name these two tribes.

    a. Reuben and Simeon
    b. Ephraim and Manasseh
    c. Gad and Asher

20. How many books are there in the Bible?

   a. 39

   b. 5

   c. 63

21. The Persian queen, wife of King Ahasueros, refused to appear before the king at a banquet as commanded, and the king

   a. beheaded her

   b. divorced her

   c. forgave her

22. Of the Twelve Tribes, Moses conferred the honor of serving as priests upon one of them. Which one?

   a. the Tribe of Judah

   b. the Tribe of Levi

   c. the Tribe of Reuben

23. The Book of Tobit is part of the

   a. Apocrypha

   b. Torah

   c. Talmud

24. Ur of the Chaldees, an ancient Babylonian city, was the home of a well-known bibli-

cal character before his departure for Haran. What was the name of this person?

   a. Joshua
   b. Abraham
   c. Moses

25. The wife of Moses was the daughter of Jethro, a priest of Midian. Her name is

   a. Dinah
   b. Deborah
   c. Zipporah

26. The insignia of Yale University has two Hebrew words on it, which according to the Bible were inscribed on the breastplate of the High Priest. What are these words?

   a. *matzo* and *maror*
   b. *urim* and *tumim*
   c. *shalom* and *beracha*

27. Jacob didn't see one of his sons for many years. He thought his son was dead. Then, news came that he was alive. And Jacob said: "My son is yet alive. I will go see him before I die."

Who was the son and why did Jacob think he was dead?

    a. The son was Simeon. Jacob thought he died in prison

    b. The son was Joseph. Jacob's sons told him that Joseph was dead

    c. The son was Isaac. He was to be offered as a sacrifice

28. Ruth, the daughter-in-law of Naomi in the Book of Ruth, was born a

    a. Jewess

    b. Moabitess

    c. Persian

29. In addition to the *Song of Songs, Lamentations, Ecclesiastes* and *Esther*, one of the following is the fifth book in the group called the Five Scrolls. Which is it?

    a. Ruth

    b. Judith

    c. Tobit

30. Saul, the first king of Israel, was succeeded by David who was his

    a. father

    b. son-in-law

    c. uncle

31. Which one of these people is *not* mentioned in the Bible?

    a. Ruth
    b. Joshua
    c. Daniel
    d. Akiba
    e. Korah

32. The Book of Leviticus (25:8) speaks of the 50th year as a special year in which slaves are freed and all land purchases of the previous 50 years must be returned to the original owner. The name of this year is

    a. the Shemitah Year
    b. the Jubilee Year
    c. the Leap Year

33. A number of events in the Bible took forty days, forty nights, or forty years. Which of the following is *not* correct?

    a. Moses was on Mount Sinai for forty days and forty nights to receive the Ten Commandments
    b. The rain fell for forty days and forty nights when Noah was in the ark
    c. Moses appeared before Pharaoh for forty days and forty nights

34. Which one of these books is *not* part of the Torah?

    a. Genesis
    b. Exodus
    c. Numbers
    d. Jeremiah

35. Pharaoh commanded that all newborn boys of the Israelites should be drowned in the Nile River. The mother of Moses wanted to save her son, so she decided to hide him. Where did she hide him?

    a. in the Temple in Jerusalem
    b. behind a tree in the Garden of Eden
    c. in a basket among the bulrushes

36. An ancient people mentioned several times in the Bible, and very hostile to the children of Israel were the

    a. Pharisees
    b. Amalekites
    c. Sadducees

37. Which one of these books is *not* part of the Prophets?

    a. Isaiah
    b. Leviticus
    c. Amos
    d. Hosea

38. Which one of the following people is not mentioned in the Bible?

    a. Daniel
    b. Balaam
    c. Elisha
    d. Hillel

39. Moses had difficulty speaking because he was tongue-tied. God told Moses to take someone along to do the talking when he appeared before Pharaoh. Who was it?

    a. Jethro, his father-in-law
    b. Amram, his father
    c. Aaron, his brother

40. Abraham had two wives who are mentioned in the Bible. One was Sarah and the other was Hagar. Each had a son. Sarah's son was Isaac. What was the name of Hagar's son?

    a. Ishmael
    b. Samuel
    c. Esau

41. Which one of these people lived first?

    a. Esau
    b. Joseph
    c. Abraham
    d. Adam

42. A book of the Bible begins: "There lived a man in the land of Uz whose name was . . . . There were born to him seven sons and three daughters. . . . His property was 7,000 sheep, 3,000 camels, 500 yoke of oxen . . . and a very large household of slaves." What was the name of this man?

    a. Amos
    b. Job
    c. Isaiah

43. Who said the following, and to whom was it said?

> There hath not come a razor upon my head; for I have been a Nazirite unto God from my mother's womb. If I be shaven, then my strength will go from me and I shall become weak, and be like any other man.

    a. Samson to Delilah
    b. David to Jonathan
    c. Jonathan to Saul

44. What character in the Bible, famous for his (her) victories over the Philistines, said the following?

With the jawbone of an ass, heaps
upon heaps;
With the jawbone of an ass have
I smitten a thousand men.

    a. David
    b. Deborah
    c. Samson

45. There are four matriarchs in Judaism. Sarah, Rachel and Rebekah are three. The fourth was married to Jacob. Her name is

    a. Miriam
    b. Dinah
    c. Leah

46. There are twelve books in the Bible known as the Minor Prophets. The prophets after whom these books were named lived from the 8th to the 5th centuries B.C.E. Which *one* of these three was *not* a Minor Prophet?

    a. Ezekiel
    b. Amos
    c. Hosea

47. Which one of the following animals or insects was not involved in any of the ten plagues

visited upon the Egyptians while the Israelites
were enslaved in Egypt?

    a. caterpillars
    b. grasshoppers
    c. frogs

48. Most of the members of the Tribe of Levi
were employed in occupations connected with
the Tabernacle. They derived their livelihood
from

    a. the half-shekel that was collected
    b. the proceeds of the sale of the Urim and
       Tumim
    c. the tithes that were collected

49. A famous declaration about the age of
peace is found in chapter 2 of the Book of Isaiah.
It reads as follows:

> And they shall beat their swords
>   into plowshares
> And their spears into ———.

What is the missing word?

    a. rakes
    b. tractors
    c. pruning-hooks

50. In the Holiness Code (Leviticus, chapter 19), laws are mentioned relating to the treatment of animals. What does the Bible say about plowing the field with a team made up of an ox and a donkey?

    a. The ox should be the same size as the donkey

    b. The two should not be used together

    c. The donkey should always be harnessed on the right side of the ox

51. Many people in the Bible lived a very long time. Moses was 120 years old when he died. Noah was 950 years old. One man lived to be 969 years old. He was Noah's grandfather. What was his name?

    a. Shem

    b. Lot

    c. Methuselah

52. Shem, Ham, and Japhet are three well-known characters in the Bible. They are

    a. the sons of Abraham

    b. the sons of Noah

    c. the sons of Ishmael

53. In the fifth century B.C.E. a governor of
Judah, who had previously served as cupbearer
to the Persian king Artaxexes I, heard of the
deplorable conditions in Jerusalem and received
permission to visit the city in order to study the
situation. He was then appointed Governor of
Judah (in 444 B.C.E.). A book of the Bible
which bears his name is called the Book of

    a. Nehemiah
    b. Akiba
    c. Bar Kochba

54. In the Bible, in particular, we read of
persons who vowed not to drink intoxicating
liquor or to have their hair cut. Sometimes, parents made the vow for their children, as in the
case of Samson and Samuel. The persons who
took such vows were called

    a. Amalekites
    b. Nazirites
    c. Karaites

55. One man in the Bible was so in love with
a woman that he was willing to work for her
father for 14 years in order to win her hand

in marriage. Who was the man, and for whom did he work?

  a. David worked for Saul in order to marry Michal
  b. Jacob worked for Laban in order to marry Rachel
  c. Adam worked for Cain in order to marry Eve

56. This person was the wife of Elimelech. Her two children were named Mahlon and Chilion. Her daughter-in-law's name was Ruth. What was her name?

  a. Esther
  b. Dinah
  c. Naomi

57. A prophet who lived during the 11th and 10th centuries B.C.E. once reprimanded King David for having sent Uriah the Hittite into the front lines. Uriah was killed and David married his wife, Bathsheba. The name of the prophet was

  a. Isaiah
  b. Hillel
  c. Nathan

58. This woman's father was Jethro; her brother-in-law was Aaron; her sister-in-law was Miriam. What was her name and what was her husband's name?

   a. Her name was Zipporah and her husband was Moses
   b. Her name was Jochebed and her husband was Amram
   c. Her name was Rachel and her husband was Moses

59. A famous incident in the Book of Leviticus concerns the daughters of Zelophehad. Their father died and left no sons. They wanted to inherit their father's property. What is the biblical law in this case?

   a. Daughters could inherit only if they promised to marry within one year
   b. If a man dies without leaving a son, the daughter inherits the property
   c. If a man dies without leaving a son, his wife inherits the property

60. The first book of the Bible is Genesis. It contains many stories about famous people. Who

among the following is *not* mentioned in the first book of the Bible?

   a. Isaac
   b. Moses
   c. Esau

61. In the early pages of the Bible we are told that God planted a garden and put Adam and Eve in that garden. What was the name of the Garden?

   a. the Garden of Sodom
   b. the Garden of Eve
   c. the Garden of Eden

62. Sarah was Abraham's wife. Before her name was Sarah, she had a different name in the Bible. What was it?

   a. Sarai
   b. Saranne
   c. Shari

63. When the children of Israel travelled through the desert, a vicious tribe of nomads blocked their path and started to war against them. Who was this tribe?

   a. Hur
   b. Midian
   c. Amalek

64. Joseph had eleven brothers and one sister. Jacob was the father of all of them, but they did not have the same mother. Which of the following had the same mother?

    a. Joseph and Judah
    b. Reuben and Benjamin
    c. Benjamin and Joseph

65. Joseph's brothers decided to kill him because they were jealous of him. But one brother said, "Let us not kill him. Throw him into the pit." He planned to come back and save Joseph. Who was this brother?

    a. Reuben
    b. Judah
    c. Benjamin

66. Judah told Jacob that they could not buy food in Egypt unless a certain brother went along with them. Which brother had to go along, and why?

    a. Dan, because he was the youngest
    b. Reuben, because he was the oldest
    c. Benjamin, because he was Joseph's blood-brother

67. "My brother is a hairy man and I am smooth." Who, in the Bible, said this to his mother?

    a. Benjamin said it to Dinah

    b. Joseph said it to Leah

    c. Jacob said it to Rebekah

68. Jacob had four wives. Two of them were Rachel and Leah. Who were the other two?

    a. Sarah and Rebekah

    b. Bilhah and Zilpah

    c. Dina and Eve

69. Jacob loved one woman and was willing to work for her father for seven years in order to marry her. The girl's father fooled him. Instead of the girl he loved, he was asked to marry her sister. What was the sister's name?

    a. Sarah

    b. Zilpah

    c. Leah

70. Dina, the daughter of Leah, was mistreated by Shechem the son of Hamor. Two of her brothers were very angry when they found out. Who were they?

    a. Simeon and Levi

    b. Levi and Ephraim

    c. Judah and Isaac

71. When the Israelites were in the desert they had no water. God commanded Moses to talk to the rock and water would come forth. Moses disobeyed God. What did he do?

    a. He built a golden calf on top of the rock
    b. He hit the rock with his staff
    c. He covered the rock with sand

72. Many characters in the Bible gave gifts to others. Who gave someone a coat for a gift?

    a. Abel gave one to God
    b. Jacob gave one to Joseph
    c. Joseph gave one to Jacob

73. Two women played an important part in the life of Moses when he was a very small baby. Who were they?

    a. Jochebed and Miriam
    b. Miriam and Zipporah
    c. Jochebed and Sarah

74. Jacob had twelve sons. Benjamin, who was born near Bethlehem, was the youngest of them all. Benjamin's mother had one other son.

Who was his mother, and who was her other son?

    a. Rachel was his mother and her other son was Joseph

    b. Leah was his mother and her other son was Reuben

    c. Zilpah was his mother and her other son was Joseph

75. While in prison in Egypt, Joseph interpreted the dreams of the king's butler and baker. Soon afterward, the baker was hung and the butler was restored to his position. How did this affect Joseph's future?

    a. Joseph became the baker and was released from prison

    b. The butler told Pharaoh immediately about Joseph, and he was freed

    c. The butler told Pharaoh about Joseph, and Joseph interpreted Pharaoh's dream

76. When Moses threw his staff to the ground, it turned into a snake. Among the people watching, one very important person was present. Who was he?

    a. Jethro, the father of Moses

    b. Jochebed, the sister of Moses

    c. Pharaoh, the King of Egypt

77. Not many artists are mentioned in the Bible. In the Book of Exodus, the job of building the Tabernacle was placed in the hands of a very talented and artistic person. Who was he?

    a. Jethro
    b. Aaron
    c. Bezalel

78. Zipporah was the wife of Moses. She was also the daughter of Jethro, a priest of Midian. Moses and Zipporah had two sons. Who were they?

    a. Gershon and Eliezer
    b. Bezalel and Hur
    c. Nadab and Abihu

79. While Joseph was in prison, Pharaoh dreamed a dream that no one could interpret. Joseph was called in, and he interpreted it. What was the dream about?

    a. It was about seven lean cows and seven fat ones
    b. It was about three lean ears of corn and three fat ones
    c. It was about seven lean horses and seven fat ones

80. After the Egyptian soldiers drowned in the Red Sea, and the Israelites were saved, someone led the women in dancing and singing. The song went as follows:

> Sing to the Lord, for he has gloriously
>   triumphed;
> The horse and the rider has he thrown
>   into the sea.

Who was the leader?

a. Aaron, the brother of Moses
b. Zipporah, the wife of Moses
c. Miriam, the sister of Aaron

81. Moses tried to persuade Pharaoh to free the children of Israel. Pharaoh promised, time and again, that he would free them, but he didn't keep his promise. After ten plagues, Pharaoh finally let them go. Which was the tenth plague?

a. the plague of blood
b. the plague of the first born
c. the plague of darkness

82. Take thou thy son thy only son, whom thou lovest and go to Mount Moriah and offer him as a sacrifice.

In this verse from the Bible, who was talking to whom?

    a. God to Abraham
    b. Abraham to Isaac
    c. God to Jacob

83. When Moses went up to Mount Sinai to receive the Ten Commandments, he didn't return for forty days and forty nights. The Israelites thought he would never come down. They asked Aaron to make a God for them. What did Aaron make?

    a. He made a holy ark
    b. He made a tabernacle
    c. He made a golden calf

84. The last five of the Ten Commandments starts with the words, "Thou shalt not. . . ." Which of the following is *not* one of these commandments?

    a. Thou shalt not work on the Sabbath
    b. Thou shalt not steal
    c. Thou shalt not covet

85. Important events happened to certain biblical characters in some unusual places. To

whom did something happen near a burning bush?

   a. Isaac
   b. Moses
   c. Joseph

86. Father and son went to Mount Moriah. The son said: "Here is the fire and wood, but where is the ram for the sacrifice?" The father answered: "God will provide it." Who was the father and who was the son?

   a. Abraham was the father and Isaac was the son
   b. Jacob was the father and Esau was the the son
   c. Abraham was the father and Jacob was the son

87. Three brothers are mentioned in the Bible. They were not very famous, but Noah, their father, was. Who were his three sons?

   a. Shem, Ham and Japheth
   b. Abraham, Isaac and Jacob
   c. Reuben, Simon and Levi

88. God promised Noah that He would not bring another flood upon the earth. The Bible

says that as a reminder of that promise we see something strange in the sky, from time to time. What is it?

    a. the sun, the moon and the stars bowing down
    b. a rainbow of many colors
    c. the face of the man in the moon

89. Cain and Abel were brothers. Cain was a farmer and Abel was a shepherd. Cain was jealous of Abel and killed him. When God asked Cain, "Where is thy brother?" what was the answer?

    a. My brother went to Dothan to see his father
    b. Am I my brother's keeper?
    c. My brother went to visit Noah

90. "Let us build a city whose top may reach the heavens." This sentence is part of a famous story with a famous name. What is the correct name?

    a. the story of the Tower of Babel
    b. the story of Jacob's Ladder
    c. the story of Pithom and Raamses

91. In the Bible, the serpent had legs like other animals. The serpent did something wrong

and as a result lost its legs and had to crawl on its belly. What did the serpent do?

    a. He told Adam that he would never have children

    b. He tempted Eve to eat of the fruit of the Tree of Knowledge

    c. He told Adam's son to cut down all the trees

92. One group of people in the Bible was punished for doing something wrong. They were trying to build a tower that would reach into heaven. What was their punishment, as the Bible describes it in the Book of Genesis?

    a. The bricks that they used fell and killed them

    b. They began to speak different languages and couldn't understand each other

    c. It rained for forty days and forty nights and they couldn't work

93. The Decalogue, meaning the "Ten Great Words," is more popularly known by another name. What is the other name?

    a. the Ten Plagues

    b. the Ten Commandments

    c. the Report of the Ten Tribes

94. The Bible is the same as

   a. the Torah
   b. the Prophets
   c. the Holy Scriptures

95. Moses performed many duties, and served the children of Israel in many ways. Which of the following, would you say, does *not* apply to Moses

   a. He was the Liberator
   b. He was the Lawgiver
   c. He was the High Priest

96. Joseph had eleven brothers, but only one was his favorite brother. Who was it and why?

   a. Reuben, because he saved him from the pit
   b. Benjamin, because they had the same mother
   c. Judah, because he was the strongest

97. When Joseph was brought to Egypt by the Ishmaelites, he was sold as a slave to an

important person in the King's court. What was the man's name, and what position did he hold?

    a. His name was Ephraim, and he was the Egyptian treasurer

    b. His name was Potifar, and he was the captain of the King's guard

    c. His name was Ishmael, and he was the King's baker

98. This woman was the sister of Aaron and Moses. She watched her infant brother when he was placed in a reed-basket on the Nile River and later, at her suggestion, Pharaoh's daughter called Moses' mother to nurse him. Her name was

    a. Zipporah
    b. Miriam
    c. Deborah

99. One of the trees in the Garden of Eden was called the Tree of Knowledge. God told Adam not to eat the fruits of the tree because, if he did, something would happen. What would happen?

    a. A rainbow would appear in the sky
    b. He would surely die
    c. He would never find his wife

100. About 2,000 years ago Jews established a correct way to spell and pronounce the Hebrew text of the Bible. This tradition became known as the

    a. Pentateuch
    b. Mishna
    c. Masorah

101. Chapter 19 in the Book of Leviticus is called the Holiness Code. Which of the following statements is a popular verse in this chapter of the Bible?

    a. Holy, holy, holy is the Lord, God of hosts
    b. Thou shalt love thy neighbor as thyself
    c. The Lord is my Shepherd, I shall not want

102. This prophet was a Judean who lived in the 8th century B.C.E. By occupation, he was a herdsman and a sycamore tree pruner. What was his name?

    a. Jeremiah
    b. Isaiah
    c. Amos

103. When Moses went up to Mount Sinai to receive the Ten Commandments he stayed away for a long time. The Israelites grew impatient,

and persuaded Aaron to build a Golden Calf
that they could worship. Where did Aaron get
the gold for the Golden Calf?

    a. He dug it out of the earth
    b. He used the doors of the Temple which
       were made of gold
    c. The women gave him their gold jewelry

104. He was King Saul's uncle and the commander of his army. After Saul's death, he became attached to the court of King David. He
was later killed by Joab. David composed a
famous lament for him. What was his name?

    a. Abner ben Ner
    b. Joshua bin Nun
    c. Akiba ben Joseph

105. The third son of King David, Absalom,
killed his half-brother Amnon because Amnon
mistreated Absalom's sister, Tamar. Absalom
then rebelled against David. Eventually he was
killed in a very strange way. How did it happen?

    a. He fell into a deep pit and suffocated
    b. He was trapped by two lions
    c. His hair became entangled in a tree

106. The third section of the Bible is called the Hagiographa (or *Ketubim*, or The Writings). Which of these Books of the Bible are part of this section?

    a. Malachi
    b. Psalms
    c. Jonah
    d. Chronicles
    e. Proverbs

107. This man was a king of Israel who ruled from about 876-853 B.C.E. His wife's name was Jezebel. Who was he?

    a. Saul
    b. Ahab
    c. David

108. This woman became King David's wife after the death of her husband, Nabal. She won David's pardon for Nabal's boorishness by her pleadings and her gifts. This woman's name was

    a. Abigail
    b. Naomi
    c. Esther

109. Abraham's intended offering of Isaac as a sacrifice in the Book of Genesis is known in Hebrew as the

    a. *Akeda*
    b. *Matan Torah*
    c. *Mabul*

110. The Book of Lamentations is read in the synagogue on

    a. Yom Kippur
    b. Purim
    c. Tishah B'Av

111. Sodom and Gomorrah are mentioned in the Book of Genesis. What are they?

    a. They are the names of people
    b. They are the names of cities
    c. They are the names of tribes

112. Samson killed the Philistines with the jawbone of an ass. How did the son of Jesse kill his opponent?

    a. with a bow and arrow
    b. with a sword
    c. with a slingshot

113. Which of these statements is true and which is false?

   a. Adam and Eve ate an apple
   b. Jonah was swallowed by a whale
   c. Mordecai was Esther's uncle

114. The burning bush, described in the Book of Exodus, was unusual because

   a. it provided Moses with light to read by for 40 nights
   b. it burned, but was not consumed
   c. it was the spot where the Ten Commandments were given

115. The book of the Bible called the Song of Songs is also referred to as

   a. Ecclesiastes
   b. Canticles
   c. Chronicles

116. "Is your father alive?" "Do you have another brother?" Who asked these questions of whom?

   a. Joseph's brothers asked Potifar
   b. Joseph asked his brothers
   c. Pharaoh asked Joseph

117. The Ten Commandments appears twice in the Bible. It appears for the first time in the Book of Exodus (Chapter 20), and then, once again, with slight variations in the

a. Book of Isaiah
b. Book of Kings
c. Book of Deuteronomy

118. Christian and Jewish tradition do not agree about the Ten Commandments. One of the differences is that Christians

a. do not consider the first verse as a commandment, and add one about the trinity
b. do not consider the first as a commandment, and divide the second into two commandments
c. do not consider the first verse a commandment, and add one about communion

119. The Latin phrase *creatio ex nihilo* refers to which of the following portions of the Bible?

a. the first chapter of Exodus
b. the first chapter of Genesis
c. the first chapter of Chronicles

120. In American history, the pilgrims were among the first to land on American shores in

the 17th century. The Bible also speaks of pilgrims. Who were they?

   a. They were the first Hebrews to enter
      Egypt after Joseph became assistant to
      the King
   b. They were the first group to enter Pal-
      estine, under Joshua, after the death of
      Moses
   c. They were those Jews who visited the
      Temple in Jerusalem on Passover, Pen-
      tecost, and Tabernacles

121. The prophet in the kingdom of Israel
during the reign of King Ahab and Queen Jezebel (9th century B.C.E.) was known as "the
Tishbite." He is mentioned prominently during
the Passover seder service. His name is

   a. Elijah
   b. Elisha
   c. Jeremiah

122. The biblical ceremony which is performed when a man refuses to marry his brother's childless widow requires that the widow
remove her brother-in-law's shoe and say "so
shall be done to the man who will not build his

brother's house." The Hebrew word for this ceremony, which means "taking off," is

   a. *hamotzi*
   b. *halitzah*
   c. *hallel*

123. The third section of the Bible which includes such books as Proverbs, Psalms, Job, and the Song of Songs is called *Ketuvim* in Hebrew, and means "Holy Writings." The Greek word for it often used, is

   a. Deuteronomy
   b. Chronicles
   c. Hagiographa

124. Ishmael, in the Bible, was the oldest son of Abraham. He was the brother of Isaac. Ishmael's mother's name was

   a. Sarah
   b. Hagar
   c. Rebecca

125. One of the characters in the Bible had three friends. They were Eliphaz the Temanite, Bildad the Shuhite and Zophar the Naamathite. This character's name was

   a. Joshua
   b. Jeremiah
   c. Job

126. Hananiah, Mishael and Azariah were friends of a person to whom strange experiences happened in the court of Nebuchadnezzar during the Babylonian exile. The name of this person was

    a. Nehemiah
    b. Ezra
    c. Daniel

127. An Israelite judge mentioned in the Book of Judges led his people in battle against the Ammonites. He vowed that if he returned safely, he would sacrifice the first thing that came out of his house. Upon his return, he was met by his daughter, whom he then sacrificed in keeping with his vow. The name of the judge was

    a. Jephthah
    b. Joshua
    c. Samson

128. In Chapter 11 of Leviticus, certain types of fish are described as kosher (fit to eat) and certain as unkosher. What makes a fish kosher?

    a. If it has fins, it is kosher
    b. If it has scales, it is kosher
    c. It must have fins and scales to be kosher

129. Samson is generally assumed to be the strong man of the Bible. Who else in the Bible was so strong that he was able, single handedly, to roll a huge stone from the mouth of a well so that his future wife might fetch some water?

    a. Joshua
    b. Jacob
    c. Joseph

130. Mount Moriah is the mountain on which Abraham was prepared to sacrifice his son Isaac. According to Jewish tradition that place is now located on the Temple Mount

    a. where the Dome of the Rock is now situated
    b. where the Hadassah hospital is now situated
    c. where the Hebrew University is now situated

131. Jacob was told that one of his sons was attacked and killed by a wild animal. Which of his 12 sons was reported killed?

    a. Benjamin
    b. Judah
    c. Joseph

132. Some people in the Bible were given names that reflected some particular happening in their lives. Moses (Moshe) was so named because

a. he was the liberator of his people
b. he brought ten plagues on Pharaoh
c. he was drawn out of water

133. Among the most famous biblical personalities who knew the secret of interpreting
dreams were
a. Joseph and David
b. Daniel and Joseph
c. David and Solomon

134. Daniel's three friends were thrown into the
lions den, but they came out unharmed. Their
Babylonian names were Shadrakh, Meshakh,
and Abed Nego, but their original Hebrew names
were
a. Hananiah, Mishael, and Azariah
b. Haim, Moshe, and Abraham Nathan
c. Shlomo, Moshe, and Adam Nathan

Holidays, Laws and
Ceremonies

Part V – HOLIDAYS, LAWS AND CEREMONIES

1. Lag Ba-Omer is a minor holiday which, according to tradition, is the day on which the plague among the students of Rabbi Akiba ended. During what season of the year does it occur in America?

    a. winter
    b. spring
    c. summer

2. The ceremony called *bedikat chametz* in Hebrew, means "the search for leaven." It is performed just prior to the

    a. Passover holiday
    b. Purim holiday
    c. Chanukah holiday

3. The word *Shaddai* (meaning "God") appears on one of the ceremonial objects used by Jews. The object is called a

    a. mezuzah
    b. kiddush cup
    c. breastplate

4. According to Jewish law, when naming a newborn baby it is

    a. not permissible to name him after a living grandfather

    b. not permissible to name him after a living grandmother

    c. permissible to name him after anyone, living or dead

5. *Minhag Ashkenaz, minhag Polin, minhag Seforad* refer to various types of

    a. ritual practice

    b. institutions of learning

    c. charitable institutions

6. The words *Machzor, Piyyut* and *Amida* are all connected in some way with

    a. Jewish philosophy

    b. Jewish art

    c. Jewish liturgy

7. The Haggadah, the Machzor and the Siddur have one thing in common. They are types of

    a. Bibles

    b. food

    c. prayerbooks

8. The holiday on which it is mandatory to eat *maror*, because it is an important symbol, is

   a. Chanukah
   b. Succos
   c. Passover

9. Rosh Hashanah is a holiday that occurs on the first day of the Hebrew month of

   a. Tishri
   b. Elul
   c. Nisan

10. We often refer to the Oral Law and the Written Law. To what does the Written Law refer?

   a. the Torah
   b. the Talmud
   c. the Kabbalah

11. *Yaaleh v'yavo* are the first words of a special prayer recited as part of the "Amida" and "Grace After Meals," on certain special days. Which days?

   a. Rosh Hashanah and Yom Kippur
   b. Rosh Chodesh and Holidays
   c. Chanukah and Purim

12. *Bikur cholim* is one of the most important commandments in Judaism. It means

    a. burying the dead
    b. honoring one's father and mother
    c. visiting the sick

13. The triennial cycle refers to a system of reading the Torah that was once used in Palestine. According to this system it

    a. took three years to read the entire Torah
    b. took three years to read all the Prophets
    c. took three years to give all men an *aliyah*

14. At the end of a wedding ceremony, the bridegroom breaks a glass. The reason usually given for this ceremony is that it is a

    a. reminder of the destruction of the Temple
    b. symbol of the breaking of the groom's ties with his family
    c. reminder that one's cup of life can never be full

15. More wine is drunk on one particular holiday than on all others. Which is it?

    a. Passover
    b. Purim
    c. Chanukah

16. The circumcision ceremony is known as the *brith* (sometimes pronounced, *bris* or *brit*). It is performed by the *Mohel* on the

    a. ninth day after the birth of a baby boy
    b. seventh day after the birth of a baby girl
    c. eighth day after the birth of a baby boy

17. The Hebrew name for Israel's Independence Day, which occurs each year on the fifth day of the Hebrew month Iyar, is

    a. *Yom Hazikaron*
    b. *Yom Hadin*
    c. *Yom Ha-atzmaut*

18. The *tefilin*, or phylacteries, which are worn by boys over the age of 13, contain four hand-written portions from the Bible. The original source of these passages is

    a. the Books of Exodus and Deuteronomy
    b. the Books of Genesis and Exodus
    c. the Books of Isaiah and Jeremiah

19. *Yizkor* is a Hebrew prayer for the dead recited in most synagogues (not in Sephardic synagogues) on the last day of the three festivals

and on the Day of Atonement. What are these three holidays?

    a. Rosh Hashanah, Pesach and Succos
    b. Pesach, Shavuos and Rosh Hashanah
    c. Pesach, Succos and Shavuos

20. One of the three pilgrim-festivals begins on the fifteenth day of Tishri each year, and is called

    a. Pesach
    b. Succos
    c. Shavuos

21. On which holiday do we *not* drink wine?

    a. Chanukah
    b. Yom Kippur
    c. Purim

22. On which holiday do we read the story of Haman?

    a. Chanukah
    b. Purim
    c. Lag B'Omer

23. Which one of these holidays does *not* come out in the same Hebrew month?

 a. Rosh Hashanah
 b. Yom Kippur
 c. Succos
 d. Purim

24. The meat of an animal like a cow or a sheep is kosher. It can be eaten, according to the dietary laws, only if it is

 a. properly slaughtered, salted and washed off
 b. properly slaughtered and salted
 c. properly slaughtered and washed off

25. According to the Book of Leviticus the only types of fish that are kosher are those that have fins and scales. Such fish can be eaten

 a. immediately
 b. after they have been slaughtered and salted
 c. after they have been properly salted and washed off

26. According to the Book of Leviticus, the first requirement for an animal to be kosher is that it must

    a. have split hooves, but need not necessarily chew its cud

    b. chew its cud, but need not necessarily have split hooves

    c. have split hooves and must chew its cud

27. According to Jewish law, a person is considered a Jew if his

    a. father and grandfather are Jewish

    b. father is Jewish, regardless of his mother's religion

    c. mother is Jewish, regardless of his father's religion

28. A *minyan*, or quorum, at which time a full religious service can be held, requires the presence of

    a. 10 men or 10 women over age 21

    b. 10 males over age 13

    c. 10 males or females over age 13

29. The Ten Days of Repentance in the Jewish calendar occur during the month of Tishri. The first day of the ten is called

    a. Rosh Hashanah
    b. Yom Kippur
    c. Tisha B'Av

30. The *Oneg Shabbat*, meaning "Sabbath delight," is a gathering held late on Saturday afternoons. It was inaugurated, in Palestine, by a well known poet and author to encourage Jews to participate in cultural activities. The man who conceived the idea was

    a. Saul Steinberg
    b. Chaim Nachman Bialik
    c. Chaim Weizmann

31. Tu Bi-Shevat is a holiday meaning the 15th day of the Hebrew month of Shevat. It is sometimes referred to as the New Year for Trees. In modern Israel it is celebrated by having school children plant trees. Another name for the holiday is

    a. Chol Ha-Moed
    b. Succos
    c. Arbor Day

32. The period of intensive mourning for the loss of a loved one is called *shivah*. *Shivah* is a Hebrew word meaning

    a. sitting
    b. sadness
    c. seven

33. The law of the Jubilee Year in the Bible concerns property that belonged to Israelites. This included the land they owned as well as their slaves. What happened on the Jubilee Year?

    a. Liberty was to be proclaimed through-out the land to all the inhabitants
    b. All slaves were freed and were given the land on which they had worked
    c. All property was returned to Moses and Aaron, who were the leaders of Israel

34. Of the major holidays mentioned in the Bible, two of them begin on the fifteenth day of the Hebrew month. Which holidays are these?

    a. Rosh Hashanah and Yom Kippur
    b. Purim and Chanukah
    c. Pesach and Succos

35. Most of the holidays are mentioned for the first time in the Book of Leviticus. Which of

the following holidays is not mentioned at all in the Bible?

    a. Tabernacles

    b. Chanukah

    c. Passover

36. Many ceremonial objects are used on different holidays. Which of the following sets of three objects all belong to one and the same holiday?

    a. matzo, lulav and esrog

    b. lulav, esrog and sukkah

    c. shofar, Torah and mezuzah

37. Pesach is Passover and Succos is Tabernacles. The third major holiday mentioned in the Book of Leviticus is sometimes called Pentecost or the Feast of Weeks. Why is it so called?

    a. Because it takes place seven weeks after Passover

    b. Because it takes place seven weeks after Purim

    c. Because it lasts for seven weeks

38. *Shacharis*, *Minchah*, and *Maariv* are the names of

    a. three Israeli newspapers

    b. three prayer services

    c. three Israeli dances

39. According to tradition, the day on which Moses came down from Mount Sinai with the second tablets of the law and discovered the Golden Calf was

   a. Yom Kippur
   b. Shavuos
   c. Chanukah

40. In the English calendar, when a leap year occurs every four years, we add one day to February making it 29 days long. On leap years that occur in the Jewish calendar

   a. we add two days to the month Tishri
   b. we add a whole month, called Adar II
   c. we subtract one day from the month of Adar

41. *Adloyada* is the name of a celebration that takes place on which holiday in Israel?

   a. Purim—It's a Purim carnival
   b. Passover—It's a model seder
   c. Chanukah—It's a menorah lighting ceremony

42. A woman whose husband has disappeared, and it cannot be proven that he is living

or dead, is not permitted to re-marry. She is called

   a. a *kalah*
   b. a *chalitzah*
   c. an *agunah*

43. *Al chet* is part of the prayers of one of the important Jewish holidays. Which one?

   a. Rosh Hashanah
   b. Pesach
   c. Yom Kippur

44. *Tishah B'av*, which commemorates the destruction of the First and Second Temples, has much in common with one of the following holidays because of the manner in which it is observed. Which one?

   a. Passover
   b. Purim
   c. Yom Kippur

45. A *Baal Koray* (sometimes pronounced *Baal Keriah*) is a person who is expert at

   a. ritual slaughtering
   b. reading the Torah
   c. building synagogues

46. The ceremony at which time sins are symbolically cast into a river is called

   a. *havdalah*
   b. *kiddush*
   c. *tashlich*

47. The long gown with a waist girdle worn by Oriental and East European Jews is called a

   a. *kaftan*
   b. *arba kanfos*
   c. *talis*

48. The ceremony of initiation for a Jewish boy occurs on the eighth day after his birth. It is called circumcision and marks his initiation into "the covenant of Abraham." The Hebrew phrase for the ceremony is

   a. *pidyon haben*
   b. *b'rith milah*
   c. *b'nai b'rith*

49. *Cholent, chremzel, chrain, gehakte leber, gribenes, kichlach,* and *tayglach* are all types of Jewish

   a. ceremonies
   b. foods
   c. religious clothing

50. The *shtreimel*, the *sheitel* and the *gartel* refer to

    a. types of food
    b. articles that are worn by men or women
    c. types of literature

51. "Maoz Tzur," is a well-known Hebrew hymn that was composed in the 13th century. In English it is known as "Rock of Ages." It is sung by Ashkenazic Jews after

    a. eating the *afikomon* on Passover
    b. eating blintzes on Shavuos
    c. lighting the Chanukah candles

52. The home ceremony which marks the end of the Sabbath consists of the recitation of special prayers over a cup of wine at which time spices and a candle are used. The Hebrew word for the ceremony is

    a. *havdalah*
    b. *besomim*
    c. *shabbos*

53. The number of people given an *aliyah* during the Torah reading is not always the same on all occasions. On Sabbath seven *aliyos* are

distributed, but on holidays that fall on a week-day only

    a. three are given

    b. five are given

    c. six are given

54. Wine plays an important role in Jewish life, but two groups mentioned in the Bible refrained from drinking wine. Who were they?

    a. the Nazirites and Rechabites

    b. the Pharisees and Sadducees

    c. the Ashkenazim and Sephardim

55. The *Mezuzah* that is mounted on the doorpost of every Jewish home is placed on

    a. the upper section of the right doorpost, as one enters

    b. the upper section of the right doorpost, as one leaves

    c. any part of the doorpost, on either side

56. The shofar which is used on Rosh Hash-anah is made of a ram's horn. The horn of a ram was selected because Abraham found a ram to use as a substitute when he was about to

    a. sacrifice his son, Isaac

    b. sacrifice his son, Ishmael

    c. circumcise his son, Esau

57. The Kol Nidre is a special prayer recited on only one holiday in the Jewish calendar. That holiday is

   a. Rosh Hashanah
   b. Yom Kippur
   c. Pesach

58. The *esrog* and *lulav* are used on Succos. An *esrog* is called a "citron" in English. What is the *lulav* called?

   a. a willow branch
   b. a myrtle branch
   c. a palm branch

59. When a boy becomes Bar Mitzvah he is called to the Torah to recite the Torah Blessings. The only time this can take place is on

   a. Saturday
   b. Saturday, Monday or Thursday
   c. any occasion when the Torah is read

60. Special foods are usually associated with a particular holiday. Which *one* of the following statements is *not* correct?

   a. Latkes are eaten on Chanukah
   b. Honey is eaten on Rosh Hashanah
   c. Blintzes are eaten on Purim

61. The *dreidel* has been used for many years to play a game on Chanukah. Four Hebrew letters appear on the sides of the *dreidel*. One is a *nun;* another is a *gimmel;* a third is a *hay.* What is the fourth letter?

    a. a *daled*
    b. an *aleph*
    c. a *shin*

62. On the Purim holiday the biblical story of Esther is read. The story is hand-lettered, on a special parchment scroll called a Megillah, and is read in the synagogue after the service on

    a. Purim eve
    b. Purim morning
    c. Purim evening and morning

63. During the reading of the Megillah on Purim, whenever the name of Haman is mentioned, it is customary to make noise. The instrument usually used for this purpose is called a

    a. dreidel
    b. shofar
    c. grogger

64. The special dessert that is served as the last food eaten at the Passover Seder meal is called the

    a. *charoses*
    b. *afikomon*
    c. *maror*

65. One of the Five Scrolls (Megillot) is called Ruth. It is the story of a Moabite girl who embraced Judaism. On what holiday is it read in the synagogue and why?

    a. On Passover, because it is the holiday when the Jews won their freedom
    b. On Shavuos, because it is the holiday on which the Jews accepted the Torah
    c. On Chanukah, because it is the holiday on which a tyrant was defeated

66. Rosh Hashanah is called the Jewish New Year. Another Jewish holiday is referred to as "New Year for Trees." What is the Hebrew name of this holiday, and when does it occur in the Jewish calendar?

    a. Succos—on the 15th day of Tishri
    b. Tisha B'av—on the 9th day of Av
    c. Chamishah Asar BiShevat—on the 15th day of Shevat

67. To which one of the following are the words *talis* and *arba kanfos* most closely assosociated?

    a. *etz chaim*
    b. *tefilin*
    c. *tzitzis*

68. Which of these songs is sung on Passover at the Seder table?

    a. Adon Olam
    b. Chad Gadyo
    c. Maoz Tzur

69. During the marriage ceremony the bride and groom stand under a canopy, while the ceremony is conducted. What is the Hebrew word for canopy?

    a. *chupah*
    b. *kesubah*
    c. *kallah*

70. In connection with the performance of what ceremony are the following words used: *K'vater, Sandek* and *Mohel?*

    a. the *bris* ceremony
    b. the *havdalah* ceremony
    c. the marriage ceremony

71. In connection with what holiday are the following words associated: *Hadasim, Aravos, S'chach* and *Pitom?*

    a. In conection with Yom Kippur
    b. In connection with Purim
    c. In connection with Succos

72. When a man or a woman is converted to Judaism, one of the rituals he or she must undergo is
    a. to be immersed in a pool of natural water
    b. to drink a cup of wine
    c. to get an *aliya* in a synagogue

73. The partition that separates the men from the women in an Orthodox synagogue is called
    a. a *mechitza*
    b. a *chutzpah*
    c. an *aliyah*

74. The Knesset in Israel, like the Congress of the United States, enacts the laws of the country. In the early history of the Jewish people, the group that made the laws was
    a. the Yishuv
    b. the Sanhedrin
    c. the United Jewish Appeal

75. The *shofar* was used in biblical times during periods of war and in times of crisis. Two

leaders who used the *shofar* effectively against an enemy were
   a. Joshua and Gideon
   b. Abraham and Isaac
   c. Moses and Aaron

76. Shushan Purim is the day on which the Jews of Shushan (capital of ancient Persia) celebrated their victory over Haman, who planned to exterminate them. The Hebrew month in which this is celebrated is
   a. Adar
   b. Sivan
   c. Tishri

Art, Entertainment
and Sports

Part VI

ART, ENTERTAINMENT AND SPORTS

1. When John J. McGraw was manager of the old New York Giants baseball team, he searched the minor leagues for a "Jewish Babe Ruth." He was anxious to attract Jews to the Polo Grounds. He thought he found the right man playing in El Paso, Texas. The player's name is

    a. Sandy Koufax
    b. Hank Greenberg
    c. Andy Cohen

2. Only one Jewish player ever won a Major League batting crown. It happened in 1935 while he was playing for the Washington Senators. That year he batted .349 and played second base. His name was

    a. Charles "Buddy" Myer
    b. Moe Berg
    c. Albert "Dolly" Stark

3. In a Broadway play called *A Majority of One*, the actress who became famous for creating and acting in the radio and TV program called *The Goldbergs* falls in love with a Japanese financier, but refuses to marry him because of their difference in religion. The name of the actress is

a. Gertrude Stein
b. Sophie Tucker
c. Gertrude Berg

4. A well-known entertainer who died in 1950 was the son of a Cantor. His first musical sound picture was called *The Jazz Singer*, in which he plays the part of a Cantor. He is best remembered for his rendition of the song "Mammy" which he sang with his face blackened. His name is

a. Eddie Cantor
b. Al Jolson
c. George Jessel

5. One of the basketball "greats" of the 20th century played professionally for the original Celtics and later became coach of the City College of New York. He coached the C.C.N.Y. teams for almost 40 years, up until 1960. He is responsible for helping establish basketball as a major sport in Israel during a 1949 visit to

that country. Often referred to as "Mr. Basketball," his real name is

   a. Barney Ross
   b. Nat Holman
   c. Harry Henshel

6. A play that tells the story of a mixed marriage had one of the longest runs on Broadway. It is a love story of a Jewish boy and a gentile girl, and has a happy ending. The play is called

   a. Funny Girl
   b. Abie's Irish Rose
   c. Hello Dolly

7. Many entertainers have been attracted to Judaism and have converted. Which one of the following is a Jewish convert?

   a. Jerry Lewis
   b. Louis "Satchmo" Armstrong
   c. Johnny Mathis

8. A great Jewish philanthropist who made a fortune in the glove business in Gloversville, N. Y., was the first Harvard football coach (in 1881), and the first Jewish collegiate coach. He served as a U.S. Congressman, representing New York, from 1898-1907. At Harvard he established the first Chair of Jewish Literature

and Philosophy ever to be established at any American university. His name is

a. Stephen S. Wise
b. Lucius N. Littauer
c. Mark Wischnitzer

9. In 1932, in Tel Aviv, more than 2,000 Jewish athletes gathered from 22 countries to participate in an all-Jewish sports spectacular. It was conducted on the style of the Olympics, and was called

a. Kaduree
b. Jewish Olympics
c. Maccabiad

10. Most comedians perform on stage, but this one (who was once a baseball pitcher) has performed many times on the baseball diamond, before regular games and before World Series games. Sometimes called "The Clown Prince of Baseball," his real name is

a. George Burns
b. Al Schacht
c. George Jessel

11. This Hungarian composer (1887-1951) settled in the United States in 1909. Among the 2,000 songs he wrote were, "The Student

Prince," "The Desert Song," and "New Moon."
His name is

    a. Sigmund Romberg
    b. Oscar Hammerstein
    c. Al Jolson

12. An American film producer who came to
the U.S. from Hungary in 1888 founded the
Paramount Picture Corporation in 1917. His
name is

    a. Spyros Skouras
    b. Jack Benny
    c. Adolph Zukor

13. Maxie Rosenblum was world light-heavy-
weight boxing champion from 1930 to 1934. He
gave up boxing in 1939 and became an entertainer. A famous nickname is attached to his
name. He is called

    a. Rosy Rosenblum
    b. King of the Ring
    c. Slapsie Maxie

14. This entertainer was born in 1889 and
died in 1966. She was a popular night-club and
musical-comedy singer and is also known for

popularizing the song "A Yiddishe Mamme."
Her name is

    a. Fannie Brice
    b. Molly Picon
    c. Sophie Tucker

15. Albert "Dolly" Stark was seen on many
baseball diamonds during his years in the Major
Leagues. What position did he hold?

    a. He was an umpire
    b. He was a coach
    c. He was a manager

16. A successful cantor at the Brooklyn Jewish Center in New York turned to opera, and
since 1945 has appeared regularly as tenor with
the Metropolitan Opera Company. His name is

    a. Richard Tucker
    b. Robert Merrill
    c. Leonard Bernstein

17. This artist was born in 1894 in the Polish
city of Lodz. He studied in Paris and became
famous for his specialization in book-illumina-
tion. He gained fame during World War II
making satirical anti-Nazi caricatures. He is
well known for his illumination of the Passover

Haggadah, and the U.S. and Israel Declarations of Independence. His name is

a. Marc Chagall
b. Ben Shahn
c. Arthur Szyk

18. A well-known TV and night club entertainer, the son of a cantor, made his Broadway debut in 1964 playing the lead in *What Makes Sammy Run?* He is married to an equally popular singer. His name is

a. Eddie Fisher
b. Steve Lawrence
c. Steve Allen

19. Irving Stone, an American novelist born in 1903, wrote novels and biographical fiction. A famous work of his called *Lust for Life* was made into a movie and is the story of

a. Rembrandt
b. Michelangelo
c. Vincent Van Gogh

20. An outstanding star half-back, who played for Columbia University from 1936-38, was elected to the College Hall of Fame. In 1939 he joined the Chicago Bears professional football

team and began to play as quarterback. He was their leading player for many years. His name is

   a. "Battling" Levinsky
   b. Sam Jaffe
   c. Sid Luckman

21. A modern artist, famous for his woodcuts on biblical and Jewish themes, became a director of the New Bezalel School of Arts and Crafts in 1933. His name is

   a. Jacob Steinhardt
   b. Menahem Ussishkin
   c. Leon Uris

22. Many Schwartzes achieved distinction. One, in particular, was an actor, a producer, and a director in the Yiddish theater. He was born in 1888 and died in 1960. His first name is

   a. Maurice
   b. Adolf
   c. Rudolf

23. Yehudi Menuhin, born in 1916, is one of the world's greatest violinists. He made his debut at the age of eight and gained world-wide renown very quickly. His younger sister is a gifted

pianist and has a very odd Biblical name. Her name is

a. Jezebel
b. Hepzibah
c. Kerenhappuch

24. Not too many Major Leaguers have hit four or more grand-slam home runs in one season. One of these was a Jewish star who played for the N. Y. Giants in 1948 and for the Boston Braves in 1950. In 1950 he hit four home runs with the bases full. His name is

a. Ed Kranepool
b. Sid Gordon
c. Vic Raschi

25. The four Marx brothers: Leonard (Chico), Arthur (Harpo), Julius (Groucho), and Herbert (Zeppo), were

a. baseball players
b. concert pianists
c. a comedy team

26. One of the most famous collegiate quarterbacks of all time was Benny Friedman. When Grantland Rice picked his All-American team for *Collier's* magazine in 1925, he had difficulty

choosing between Friedman and Red Grange of
the University of Illinois. For what college team
did Benny Friedman play from 1924-26?

    a. New York University
    b. University of Michigan
    c. Columbia University

27. A well-known family of Yiddish actors
began its career when its first member acted in
Russia in 1878. They also appeared in London
in 1883, then in America in 1888. Since then,
members of the same family included Luther,
Sarah, and Stella. What was their family name?

    a. Skulnick
    b. Schwartz
    c. Adler

28. Abe Saperstein, who was born in London,
England in 1901, has been called the "Barnum
of Basketball." His famous all-Negro team,
which he organized and coaches, is known as the

    a. Harlem Globetrotters
    b. Black Sox
    c. Knickerbockers

29. A famous boxer who held the world light-weight championship (1934-35), and the world welterweight championship (1934-38) was

    a. Max Baer
    b. Benny Leonard
    c. Barney Ross

30. A soloist and piano recording artist of great fame arrived in the United States from Poland in 1940. He is also well-known for his piano compositions. His name is

    a. Yehudi Menuhin
    b. Artur Rubinstein
    c. Leonard Bernstein

31. A world-renowned French actress was half-Jewish. She was born in 1844 and was educated as a Catholic. In 1915 one of her legs was amputated, but she continued with her acting career until her death in 1923. Her name is

    a. Eva Marie Saint
    b. Clara Bow
    c. Sarah Bernhardt

32. Born in 1918, this American musician became permanent conductor of the New York Philharmonic Orchestra. His compositions in-

clude the *Jeremiah* symphony, *The Age of Anxiety* (Symphony No. 2), as well as musical scores for shows like *Wonderful Town, Candide* and *West Side Story.* His name is

a. Leonard Bernstein
b. Artur Rubinstein
c. Arthur Szyk

33. The first Jewish players ever to make the American Davis Cup tennis team did so in 1951. Their names are

a. Mel Allen and Bill Stern
b. Louis Finkelstein and Samuel Belkin
c. Dick Savitt and Herb Flam

34. Ernest Bloch was born in Switzerland in 1880 and moved to the United States in 1917. His major contribution to the world was in the area of

a. sculpture and painting
b. science and medicine
c. Jewish music

35. Daniel Mendoza won a sports title in England in 1792. He was the first Jew, anywhere in the world, to win such a title. The sport in which he was champion and about which he

later wrote a book containing the rules of the game, was

- a. tennis
- b. fencing
- c. boxing

36. Edward Israel Iskowitz was born in 1892 and was prominent in every phase of entertainment. He was president of the Jewish Theatrical Guild, the Screen Actors Guild, and the American Federation of Radio Artists. He is better known as

- a. Edward G. Robinson
- b. Eddie Cantor
- c. Edward R. Murrow

37. The stained-glass windows at the Hadassah Medical Center in Jerusalem are the work of the artist

- a. Ben Shahn
- b. Marc Chagall
- c. Saul Raskin

38. Jews have been great chess enthusiasts for centuries. Rashi mentions it in his writings, and it is believed that the 11th century scholar, Simeon the Great of Mayence, played the game

with a Pope. One of the greatest American chess players of all time is

   a. Adolph Schayes
   b. Benny Goodman
   c. Samuel Reshevsky

39. A famous musician, born in Germany in 1832, came to the U.S. with his family in 1871. His two sons, Walter and Frank were, like their father (whose first name was Leopold), outstanding conductors and composers. The family name is

   a. Marx
   b. Damrosch
   c. Bernstein

40. In the early part of the 20th century the Jews of Vienna organized an intensive program of physical education in Jewish schools. Out of this program the Hakoah Club developed. Members of this club competed the world over in the 1920s, and were easily recognized by the Star of David they wore on their uniforms. The sport they engaged in was

   a. soccer
   b. lacrosse
   c. basketball

41. Jascha Heifetz was born in Vilna and settled in the United States in 1917. Before the age of five, he began to make concert appearances and became one of the world's leading artists. In 1926 he donated a concert hall to Tel Aviv. The instrument at which he has shown his genius is the

   a. piano
   b. oboe
   c. violin

42. From 1901 to 1913 a Jewish catcher played with a number of clubs in the National League. He has been ranked as one of the great catchers of all time. His name is

   a. Al Rosen
   b. Johnny Kling
   c. Abe Simon

43. This American composer, born in 1898 (died in 1937), introduced jazz and the blues into symphonic music, as was effectively demonstrated in his *Rhapsody in Blue* and *American in Paris*. His *Porgy and Bess* is one of America's favorite musical plays. The lyrics of much

of his music was written by his brother Ira. The name of the composer is

    a. Leonard Bernstein
    b. George Gershwin
    c. Sol Hurok

44. This American author, born in 1915, wrote many plays including, *A View From the Bridge* and *Death of a Salesman*. He is the winner of a Pulitzer Prize. For a while he was married to Marilyn Monroe. What is his name?

    a. Norman Mailer
    b. Arthur Miller
    c. David Merrick

45. Lipman E. Pike, the son of a Brooklyn haberdasher, was born in 1845 and died in 1893. In 1866 he played ball for a team called the Philadelphia Athletics and received $20.00 per week for playing. He was the first professional

    a. football player
    b. basketball player
    c. baseball player

46. Fanny Brice was a great Jewish comedienne who achieved her greatest fame for a

character that she created. The name of that character was

    a. Little Orphan Annie
    b. Topsy
    c. Baby Snooks

47. A Hebrew theater company was established in Moscow in 1917. It was later transferred to Israel. In 1958 it took the name: Israel National Theater. Its Hebrew name means "the stage." In Hebrew it is called

    a. Hadoar
    b. Haboker
    c. Habimah

48. A Jewish sculptor born on the East Side of New York City in 1880 (died in 1959) gained international fame for his busts of leading personalities including Albert Einstein, Chaim Weizmann, Winston Churchill, Ramsay MacDonald and George Bernard Shaw. He settled in England in 1904 and was later knighted. His name is

    a. Jacob Epstein
    b. Marc Chagall
    c. Raphael Soyer

49. Hank Greenberg was born in 1911. During his career as a baseball player, he played for the Detroit Tigers and Pittsburgh Pirates. Hank was his nickname. What is his real name?

    a. Hans
    b. Heinrich
    c. Henry

50. The following artists were specialists, at one point in their careers, in *one* form of music: Yosele Rosenblatt, Moshe Koussevitsky and Richard Tucker. What they had in common was that they were all

    a. cantors
    b. opera singers
    c. composers

51. Kurt Baum, Jan Peerce and Richard Tucker are all Metropolitan Opera stars. They have one thing in common. What is it?

    a. They are all baritones
    b. They are all altos
    c. They are all tenors

52. The head coach (in 1966) of the San Diego Chargers started his football career at Ohio State University in 1931. The coach of Army, Red Blaik, said of him in 1955: "There are few

brilliant thinkers left in football. ——— ———
is one of them." His name is

    a. Sid Gillman
    b. Lon Myers
    c. Moe Berg

53. The following three women are popular
personalities in Israel as well as in the United
States: Shoshana Damari, Sarah Osnat-Halevi
and Bracha Zefira. They have all appeared on
the stage. What do they have in common?

    a. They are all Yemenite singers of Hebrew
       folk songs
    b. They are all opera singers
    c. They all play piano, dance and sing while
       performing

54. A famous American boxer who won the
world heavyweight championship in 1934 wore
boxing trunks with a Star of David on it, although he was not Jewish. He died in 1959. His
name is

    a. Benny Leonard
    b. Max Baer
    c. Barney Ross

55. Richard Tucker was a successful synagogue cantor who turned to opera in 1945 when he made his debut with the Metropolitan Opera Company in New York. Another Metropolitan soloist who also excels in cantoral music is

    a. Rudolf Bing
    b. Jan Peerce
    c. Steve Lawrence

56. In what sport did Edward Gottlieb and Harry D. Henshel earn their reputations? Gottlieb was born in 1900. Henshel was born in 1890.

    a. football
    b. basketball
    c. baseball

57. Match these outstanding college basketball players with the college teams they played for. Which of these is correct?

    a. Barry Kramer played for Duke University
    b. Art Heyman played for New York University
    c. Rudy Larusso played for Dartmouth

58. Match these Jewish players to the sports in which they excelled. Which is correct?

    a. Vic Hershkowitz excelled in baseball
    b. Cal Abrams excelled in handball
    c. Abe Segal excelled in tennis

59. This one-time player has been called the greatest professional basketball coach of all time. His team won the National Basketball Asciation title eight consecutive times from 1959-66. Among the most prominent players who played on his team were Bob Cousy and Bill Russel. This coach's name is

    a. Mel Allen
    b. Arnold "Red" Auerbach
    c. Bernard "Red" Sarachek

60. Cecil M. Hart (1883-1940) was a Canadian. He was a descendant of Aaron Hart, the first Jew to settle in Canada. Although in his early years he was completely absorbed in baseball, he is best known for his connection with another sport. The Hart Trophy is presented annually to the most valuable player in this sport. What is the name of the sport?

    a. baseball
    b. basketball
    c. hockey

61. This young ball player was voted the Most Valuable Player and Rookie of the Year in the International League in 1965. In 1966 he won the Topps Award for being the outstanding Minor League player and led his league in home runs (29) and runs batted in (102). His name is

   a. Al Rosen
   b. Vic Raschi
   c. Mike Epstein

62. One of the most popular movie actresses of stage and screen converted to Judaism. Her name is

   a. Joan Crawford
   b. Liv Ullman
   c. Elizabeth Taylor

63. One of the most versatile entertainers of stage and screen was converted to Judaism. His name is

   a. Jack Benny
   b. Sammy Davis, Jr.
   c. Jack Lemmon

64. One of these black baseball players married a Jewish girl and converted to Judaism. His name is

   a. Hank Aaron
   b. Rod Carew
   c. Jackie Robinson

65. The famous school in Israel that specializes in teaching physical education and sports is
   a. the ORT school in Jerusalem
   b. the Orte Wingate School in Netanya
   c. Ben-Gurion University in Beersheba

66. Mark Spitz won more gold medals at the 1972 Olympics than any other athlete—five of them. Mark is a champion
   a. tennis player
   b. swimmer
   c. boxer

67. Jan Peerce, Richard Tucker, and Yossele Rosenblatt had one thing in common. All of them
   a. sang the lead role in *Fiddler on the Roof*
   b. officiated at High Holiday services as cantors
   c. preached sermons in synagogues

Answers

PART I—Persons and Places

Answers to questions on pages 3-50

1. Emanuel Celler is a Congressman from New York. He was never a Senator. Jacob K. Javits didn't begin serving as Senator until after 1957. Neither of the two was ever Governor. The correct answer is Herbert H. Lehman.
2. Asser Levy is the correct answer.
3. Abraham Mapu was an outstanding Hebrew novelist.
4. David Marcus is the correct answer. The book and movie, *Cast a Giant Shadow*, is the story of his life. Javits and Frankfurter are not professional military men.
5. The famous Rothschild family is noted for its great financial empire and the many philanthropies towards which its members have contributed.
6. Franz Rosenzweig is the correct answer. Werfel was a novelist and poet. Freud was a doctor.
7. The Uganda Scheme is the correct answer. The Balfour declaration and the White Paper were events that took place many years after Herzl's death.
8. Lillian Wald is the correct answer. Golda Meir, Prime Minister of Israel, was born at a later date. Henrietta Szold was not a social worker by profession, although she did a good deal of important social work.

9. Chaim Weizmann was a chemist by profession. He pursued his chemical studies at German and Swiss universities, and was appointed lecturer in biological chemistry at Manchester, in England. In 1916, he became director of the British Admiralty Chemical Laboratories. He gained an international reputation for his discoveries in the field of organic chemistry.

10. Treblinka was one of the notorious Nazi concentration camps.

11. Next to Bialik, Tschernichovsky was probably the greatest Hebrew poet of his time.

12. Ussishkin was an outstanding Zionist figure. A book entitled *The Mighty Warrior* is the story of his life.

13. The Touro Synagogue, a small, quaint structure, is located in Newport, Rhode Island.

14. Titus was the Roman emperor who destroyed Jerusalem after a siege of five months.

15. Albert Einstein was keenly interested in Israel scientific institutions, especially the Hebrew University, of which he was a trustee. He was offered the presidency of Israel after Weizmann's death, but preferred to continue with his scientific research.

16. The country from which Jews were expelled in 1492 was Spain.

17. Zerubabel was one of the first to return. Akiba and Maimonides lived at a much later time.

18. Yigael Yadin is the soldier-scholar who is an expert on the Dead Sea Scrolls. Morgenstern is an American scholar. Yalkut Shimoni is not a

person. It is the name of a book (a midrashic collection).

19. Charles Steinmetz, whose middle name was Proteus, is the correct answer.

20. The Israelis attacked Egypt on October 29, 1956 in order to break the ring of encirclement created by the anti-Israel alliance of Egypt, Jordan, and Syria. France and England had come to the aid of Israel by bombing strategic Egyptian positions, but the pressure brought to bear by the United States caused France and England to withdraw, and Israel to evacuate the Gaza Strip, which it had captured.

21. Titus was a Roman Emperor. The Arch of Titus is in Rome.

22. Avraham Stern, whose pseudonym was Yair, was the head of the Stern Gang which was the most militant anti-British group in the 1940's. Isaac Stern was a genius at the violin. He made his debut at the age of 11. Otto Stern was a physicist. In 1933 he was appointed research professor of physics at the Carnegie Institute of Technology in Pittsburgh, Pa.

23. Weizmann and Ben Gurion were not archaeologists.

24. The correct answer is Hyman George Rickover. Walter Shirra is an astronaut. Mickey Marcus was a soldier.

25. Pithom and Raamses were the names of these cities. Sodom and Gomorrah were important cities in the days of Abraham. Gad and Asher were the sons of Jacob.

26. Isaac and Raphael Soyer gained reputations as artists.

27. Baruch Spinoza is the correct answer. Crescas was a Spanish philosopher who lived in the 14th century. Joseph Caro was a 16th century legalist, not a philosopher.

28. Moses Alexander and Arthur Seligman served as Governors. Javits was elected Senator from New York.

29. The Geniza fragments were discovered in a synagogue in Cairo, Egypt.

30. Bela Schick discovered the Schick Test to determine one's susceptibility to diphtheria.

31. Ilya Schor as an accomplished artist and silversmith.

32. A Jew who was given special privileges was called a *hofjude*, meaning "Court Jew." *Hofjuden* (plural) served as financial agents in behalf of rulers in Central and Eastern Europe during the 17th and 18th centuries.

33. Brandeis was appointed by President Wilson in 1916, and served until his retirement in 1939.

34. Amos and Zechariah were prophets, and each has a book in the Bible named after him, which describe his prophesies. Rashi was a Bible commentator who lived about 1500 years after these prophets.

35. Of these five people Jonah is the only person mentioned in the Bible, so obviously he lived first.

36. Schiff was a great philanthropist who was born after the American revolution. He was born in Germany in 1847. Edmond Rothschild was also

a philanthropist who lived from 1845-1935. The correct answer is Haym Salomon.

37. Jonas Salk discovered a vaccine to prevent polio.

38. Rabbi Solomon ben Isaac is better known as Rashi. He was a French rabbinical scholar (born in 1040 and died in 1105).

39. The name of the city was Pumbedita.

40. As a result of Luther's revolution the condition of the Jews became worse. At first he spoke favorably of the Jews, and condemned their mistreatment by the Catholic Church, hoping that they would be attracted to his views. When they refused, he began to favor persecution of the Jews of Germany.

41. Uriah P. Levy was at the forefront of the battle to abolish corporal punishment in the Navy.

42. The Governors whom the Romans sent in to rule Judea were called *Procurators*. Altogether, there were 14 Procurators in the 60 year period. The Hasmoneans and Amoraim were Jews, not Romans.

43. The country we call Iran today is the Persia of old.

44. The missing word is "dream."

45. These men were all great physicists. Michelson, an American, won the prize in 1907. Rabi, an American, won the prize in 1944. Segre, an Italian, won the prize in 1959. Bohr, a Danish half-Jew, won the prize in 1922.

46. Nehardea was a Babylonian town situated on the Euphrates River.

47. The Aramaic name for an interpreter is *Meturge-*

man. The *tanna* and the *amora* were teachers of the Law.

48. His name is Pierre Mendès-France. During his terms as premier he negotiated an armistice in Indo-China.

49. His name is Benjamin Disraeli. Alfred Dreyfus was a Frenchman. Lord Balfour lived much later, and was never Prime Minister of England. Besides, Balfour was not Jewish.

50. The name of the philosopher is Moses Maimonides. Nachmanides and Mendelssohn were also great scholars.

51. These laws were called May Laws, and were largely responsible for the wholesale Jewish emigration from Russia during that period.

52. Wasserman's most famous discovery was the "Wasserman Reaction," for diagnosing syphilis. Freud was a famous psychoanalyst. Cohn was a famous German bacteriologist and botanist of the 19th century who discovered ways of combating plant disease.

53. Her original name was Golda Meyerson.

54. These Jews were known as Marranos.

55. His name is Karl Marx. Alexander Marx was a Jewish historian. Adolph Marx was a Jewish composer.

56. Auschwitz was the name of the extermination camp.

57. Jewish scholars who lived in Palestine and Babylonia from the 3rd to the 6th centuries were called Amoraim.

58. The name of this site is Tel El Amarna.

59. His name was Aaron of Lincoln. Disraeli and Brandeis lived many centuries later and were not financiers.

60. They came from Yemen.

61. Nordau called such Jews *luftmenschen,* which means "men of the air (or spirit)."

62. Alfred Adler was a great psychologist. Julius Adler was a journalist. Cyrus Adler was the scholar.

63. His name was Akiba ben Joseph (Rabbi Akiba).

64. The king's name was Alexander.

65. The statement of Lord Balfour, which is known as the "Balfour Declaration," proved of great importance for the future establishment of the State of Israel.

66. Jacob Barsimon was the first Jewish settler in the New World.

67. Bernard Baruch was a confidential adviser to Franklin D. Roosevelt and other presidents who succeeded him.

68. Ben-Zvi, whose original name was Shimshelevitz, was a journalist and scholar. He published papers on several aspects of Jewish history, especially on the Samaritans and oriental communities.

69. Her name was Beruria.

70. Count Folke Bernadotte was the Swedish diplomat. A Jewish terrorist organization which was a splinter group of *Lohame Herut Israel* claimed responsibility for his assassination.

71. The man's name was Mordecai Manuel Noah. He was an American diplomat and author. He

was the U.S. consul to Tunis from 1813 to 1815, and later became sheriff of New York County.

72. Bethlehem is the city in which King David was born.

73. That region is called Birobidjan. Of the 20,000 Jews who went there in the early days of the experiment, 11,000 had left by 1934.

74. Ernest Bloch (1880-1959) was the composer. Felix Bloch (1905-) is a physicist. Joshua Bloch (1890-1957) was the librarian.

75. His name is Martin Buber. Among his most famous works which have appeared in English are: *I and Thou, For the Sake of Heaven,* and *Tales of the Hassidim.*

76. Buchenwald became famous because the Nazis established a concentration camp there.

77. The correct number is 40. Of this number, eight were half-Jewish. Of these eight, seven had a Jewish mother and a non-Jewish father, while one had a Jewish father and a non-Jewish mother.

78. Israel was called Canaan in the days of Moses.

79. The large depository consisted primarily of old, sacred books. The depository was called Genizah meaning "hiding," in Hebrew.

80. David Moses Cassuto is a famous Bible scholar.

81. The troopship was the *SS Dorchester.*

82. Bogdan Chmielnicki was a notorious Cossack leader responsible for the annihilation of hundreds of Jewish communities and the murder of hundreds of thousands of Jews. Only those

Jews who were willing to be baptized were spared.

83. His name is Luis de Torres. Although a Jew by birth, he was baptized immediately before Columbus' expedition set sail.

84. Manasseh ben Israel was the Dutch rabbi. Solomon Gabirol and Judah Halevi lived in a much earlier period.

85. Beersheba is the southern city.

86. Hillel, sometimes called Hillel the Elder, is the author of the Golden Rule in its negative form.

87. Senator Abraham Ribicoff was formerly the Governor of Connecticut. Javits is a Senator, and Halpern, a Congressman, both from New York State.

88. Arthur Goldberg is the correct answer.

89. Ahad Ha-am's real name was Asher Ginsberg. Louis Ginzberg was a talmudic scholar, and Jekuthiel Ginsburg was a mathematician.

90. Nelson Glueck achieved fame as an archaeologist. He is the author of *Rivers in the Desert,* a book about explorations in the Negev.

91. Samuel Loeb Gordon was a Hebrew author and Bible commentator.

92. They were all false messiahs.

93. His name is Abba Eban.

94. His name is Sigmund Freud.

95. Felix Frankfurter is the correct answer.

96. They all professed another religion outwardly but practiced Judaism secretly.

97. Medicine, first; physics, second. Sixteen of the 40 Jewish Nobel Prize winners won the award

for their achievements in medicine; thirteen, for their achievements in physics.

98. His name is David Dubinsky. He retired in 1966.

99. His name is Moses Aaron Dropsie. Abraham Neuman was the second president of the college, succeeding Cyrus Adler in 1941.

100. Vladimir Jabotinsky was the militant Zionist, although Herzl and Hess were also Zionists of an earlier period.

101. Israel Friedlaender is the correct answer. Hyamson and Schechter also taught at the Seminary. Schechter served as president as well.

102. Ludwig Lewisohn achieved distinction as a professor and author. He was a professor of German at Ohio State University from 1911 to 1948. From 1948 until his death he was professor of comparative literature at Brandeis University. Among his most famous works are *The Island Within* and *The Last Days of Shylock*.

103. Jericho is a West Bank city. Jerusalem and Haifa are not on the West Bank.

104. Yitzhak Rabin was the only Prime Minister born in Israel.

105. Golda Meir's name was Myerson. She and her husband changed it to Meir after they moved to Israel from the United States.

106. After the Sinai War of 1956, when Israel conquered the entire Sinai peninsula, President Dwight D. Eisenhower pressured Israel to return the captured territories.

107. The name of this group whose members lived pri-

marily in Nablus (the biblical city of Schechem) is Samaritans.

108. The most important people present at the Camp David summit meeting were Sadat, Begin and Carter.

109. The Jewish community in Israel was known as the Yishuv (*Yishuv* being the Hebrew word for "settlement").

110. The Jews of Ethiopia are known as Falashas. Falashas probably means "immigrants."

111. A Catholic Monastery was built at the base of Mt. Sinai in the fourth century. Its name is Santa Caterina (Saint Catherine).

112. Jews came to North America from Pernambuco, Brazil, in 1654. The first boatload of 23 people landed in New Amsterdam (New York).

113. Spinoza was excommunicated by the leaders of the Jewish community of Amsterdam, Holland, because his ideas about God were considered to be atheistic.

114. The Dome of the Rock now stands on the spot where Solomon's Temple once stood, and where the sacrifice of Isaac was to take place.

115. It was the name of a ship transporting Jewish refugees from Europe. It was not permitted to land in any port and had to return to Europe.

116. They all had the name Moshe, or Moses, as their first name.

117. Auschwitz and Bergen-Belsen were among the most notorious. Berlin and Prague were not the names of camps.

118. The Touro Synagogue is in Newport, Rhode Island.

119. The king's name was Herod.

120. Torquemada was the priest (confessor) who served the court of Queen Isabella of Spain.

121. They were all presidents of the same Orthodox seminary: The Rabbi Isaac Elchanan Theological Seminary, which is part of Yeshiva University.

122. They were all presidents of Jewish theological seminaries.

123. Ezer Weizman (spelled with one "n") was an army general, and a Minister of Defense in Begin's government.

124. His immediate predecessor was Yitzhak Rabin. He was preceded by Golda Meir. Dayan and Peres were never Prime Ministers.

125. All were presidents of The Jewish Theological Seminary of America—a Conservative seminary.

126. Vladamir Jabotinsky had the greatest influence on Begin's life.

127. Haifa is the largest port in Israel. Ashdod is second in size. Tel Aviv does not have a port.

128. He is called an *oleh*. A *sabra* is a native-born Israeli. A *shadchan* is a matchmaker.

129. *Sabra* is the Hebrew word for "cactus." Israelis in the earliest days of statehood were said to be like the cactus: tough and prickly on the outside, but soft and tender on the inside.

130. Anwar Sadat started the Yom Kippur War in 1973.

131. Gamal Abdul Nasser was Sadat's predecessor as President of Egypt.

132. Chaim Weizmann was a chemist. He was the first President of Israel, elected in 1948 by the Israeli Knesset.

133. The mystic known as The Ari was Rabbi Isaac Luria. He was born in Jerusalem and died in Safed (Tzefat) at the age of 38.

PART II—Language and Literature

Answers to questions on pages 51-84

1. "The New Colossus," is inscribed on the Statue of Liberty, which was a gift to the U.S. from France.
2. Meyer Levin is the full name of the author.
3. The correct answer is Rebecca. It is believed that she was the prototype for Sir Walter Scott's heroine in *Ivanhoe*.
4. His full name is Moses Chaim Luzzatto.
5. The story is based on the writings of Sholom Aleichem.
6. The Book of Maccabees is part of the Apocrypha which includes books of high calibre that were not admitted into the official Bible collection. The books of the Apocrypha were written, for the most part during the period of the Second Temple.
7. These are the names of popular prayers found in the prayerbook.
8. It is called *Yahrzeit*, which is the German word meaning "anniversary."
9. The correct answer is *yishuv*, which is a Hebrew word meaning "settlement."
10. The correct answer is *yichus*, which is a Hebrew word meaning "distinction."
11. The author's name is Herman Wouk.

12. The word Essene has no direct connection with the Talmud. *Bavli* and *Yerushalmi* are the Hebrew names of the Babylonian (Bavli) and Jerusalem (Yerushalmi) Talmud collections.

13. Leopold Zunz was a scholar who wrote a good deal about history, midrash and liturgy.

14. These five expressions are different ways of saying "congratulations." Sephardim use the form *be-simman tov*, which actually means "in good omen." Ashkenazim use the form *yeyasher koach* meaning "may He (God) increase your strength," for someone who has performed a religious duty, such as having been called to recite the Torah blessings. Sephardim also use the phrase *tizkeh lemitzvot* meaning "may you have the merit to perform *mitzvot*," after a religious duty has been performed. *Mazal u-veracha*, like *mazal tov*, means "good luck," or "luck and blessings."

15. He is most famous for his novel *Exodus*.

16. The author's name is Franz Werfel.

17. The name of the book is *The Last of the Just*.

18. The correct Hebrew phrase is *zechus avos*. *Pidyon haben* and *shalom zachor* are the names of ceremonies that relate to newborn baby boys.

19. His name is Moses Maimonides.

20. The correct Hebrew expression is *zichrono livrocho*. *L'chayim* is a way of saying "congratutions." *L'hitraot* means "until we meet again."

21. Emile Hertzog is the real name of the distinguished French author André Maurois. Maurois has been a member of the Académie Française since 1938.

22. Harry Austryn Wolfson is the correct answer.

23. The name of the book is *Dr. Zhivago*.

24. *Yom tov* means "good day." *Yom ha-din* means "day of judgment," and *yom teruah* "the day of blowing the *teruah*," one of the sounds of the *shofar*.

25. The correct answer is *tagin*.

26. Her name is Hanna Szenes.

27. His name is Mark W. Wischnitzer. Salo Baron wrote an introduction to the volume.

28. The name of the periodical is *Hadoar*.

29. The Hebrew name for the red heifer is *parah adumah*.

30. His name is Maurice Samuel.

31. It is called *ner tamid*.

32. The name of the river is Sambatyon.

33. The native Israeli is called a *sabra*.

34. The Hebrew term for the sacrifice of Isaac is *akeda*.

35. The Hebrew title of Saadya's famous book is *Emunot VeDeot*.

36. The name of Pinsker's pamphlet is *Auto-Emancipation*.

37. His last name is Peretz.

38. The name of the author is Joseph Opatoshu. His original name was Opatovsky.

39. His name is Moses Mendelssohn.

40. The name of the book is *History of the Jewish People*, published by the Jewish Publication Society of America.

41. His name is Sholem Asch. Asch's aim in writing books on Christian themes was to demonstrate the

common heritage of Jews and Christians. Orthodox circles, in particular, did not look with favor
upon his writings.

42. His pen-name was Mendele Mocher Sephorim.

43. The actual meaning of *am ha-aretz*, as used in
every-day talk, is "ignoramus."

44. His name is Israel Zangwill. Judah Touro and
Benjamin Disraeli were not writers.

45. Sholom (sometimes spelled Sholem) Aleichem's
real name was Shalom Rabinovich. *Fiddler on the
Roof* is based on the character of *Tevye der
Milchiger* (Tevye the Milkman).

46. Israel Abrahams wrote *Jewish Life in the Middle
Ages.*

47. *Tanach* is the Hebrew abbreviation for Bible. It
stands for *Torah, Neviim* and *Ketubim,* the three
divisions of the Bible.

48. They are called *neginot* or *te'amim.* They are also
known as *trop.*

49. *The Bridal Canopy* is a well known book by
Agnon. In 1966 he was awarded the Nobel Prize
for literature.

50. Grace Aguilar is the author of *Vale of Cedars.*

51. Asher Ginsberg's pen-name was Ahad Ha'am.

52. The Hebrew alphabet has a total of 27 letters: 22
plus 5 final letters.

53. The Hebrew word is *aliyah.*

54. *Auto-de-Fé* means "act of faith."

55. The opposite of *mitzvah* (which means "righteous
deed") is *averah* (which means "sin").

56. His name is Salo W. Baron.

57. Saul Bellow's most famous novel is *The Adventures of Augie March.*

58. Eliezer ben Yehudah is most famous for writing a comprehensive dictionary of ancient and modern Hebrew.

59. *The Wisdom of Ben Sira* is similar to the *Book of Proverbs* in the Bible. It contains wise sayings and proverbs.

60. Benjamin of Tudela began traveling about 1165. His book describes his travels to 300 different places in France, Italy, Greece, Syria, Palestine, Iraq, the Persian Gulf, Egypt and Sicily.

61. Bialik's famous poem about a yeshiva student is called "Hamasmid." He also wrote the poems entitled "Ir Ha-harega," and "Megillas Ha-esh."

62. The magazine is called *Bitzaron.*

63. *B'nai B'rith* means "sons of the covenant."

64. The high point in Léon Blum's career was reached when he became Premier of France.

65. The author of these works is Martin Buber.

66. Abraham Cahan wrote *The Rise of David Levinsky.*

67. *Av* means "father."

68. All three phrases mean "cemetery."

69. *Nachas* means "peace, pleasure, or contentment."

70. The inhabitants of Helm were noted for their naiveté.

71. The name of the French Army captain was Alfred Dreyfus.

72. All three are types of coins.

73. *Yaale v'yavo* is a Hebrew prayer found in the prayerbook. It does not mean "congratulations."

74. The Hebrew word for confession of sins is *viddui*.
75. Literally, *tzedakah* means "righteousness."
76. This author's name was Stefan Zweig.
77. The Rip Van Winkle of talmudic fame was Honi Ha-meaggel, sometimes called Choni Hamaagol.
78. *Ibn* and *bar* mean the same as *ben*. All mean "son" or "son of."
79. All three expressions mean "holidays."
80. The actual Hebrew phrase is *hillul ha-Shem. Kiddush ha-Shem* has the opposite meaning.
81. The person who chants the service is called the *hazzan*. The *baal koray* reads the Torah.
82. The automaton is called a *golem*.
83. These letters are *daled* and *hay*. An accent mark (or apostrophe is placed after the letter to indicate that it is an abbreviation. In addition to the *daled* and *hay*, the letter *yad* (or *yud*) is used in the same manner.
84. The author is Heinrich Graetz. Ismar Elbogen wrote a supplementary volume (to bring it up-to-date) entitled *A Century of Jewish Life*, which covers the period from 1840 to 1940.
85. The name of the selection is the popular *Chad Gadya*.
86. The Hebrew words mean "on high."
87. Imber's famous poem is *Hatikvah*, which became the Jewish national anthem.
88. These three phrases refer to prayers recited during the *Yom Kippur* service.
89. *The Protocols* is full of vicious lies about Jews and Judaism and is considered to be the Bible of many anti-Semites.

90. Chaim Potok wrote most of these books. Saul Bellow wrote *Herzog*. Leon Uris wrote *Exodus*.

91. Pinsker was an early Zionist who believed Jews must have a land of their own.

92. Isaac Bashevis Singer, who wrote all his stories and novels in Yiddish, won the Nobel Prize for Literature in 1978.

93. Most Yiddish words come from a German dialect called High German. This was the more literary form of German used by the more educated Germans. The language of the masses was called Low German.

94. The Hebrew name is Kotel Maaravi, *kotel* meaning "wall," and *maaravi* meaning "from the west."

95. Eastern Jews (from Spain, Italy, North Africa and Middle Eastern countries) use the sephardic pronunciation.

PART III – Institutions

Answers to questions on pages 85-104

1. It is the equivalent of the Red Cross.
2. They were Nazi extermination camps.
3. The first president of the Hebrew University was Judah Leon Magnes. Earlier, he served as rabbi of Temple Emanuel in New York City for four years.
4. The name Mapai means "Israel Workers' Party." It is a labor party that was created in 1930 as a result of a merger of Ha-Poel Hatzair and Ahdut Ha-Avodah. By 1935 it became the strongest party in the Zionist Organization. In the 1959 election Mapai received 55.43% of the votes.
5. The institute is known as *ulpan*. The Hebrew word *ulpan* means "study."
6. It was called Youth Aliyah, which was responsible for saving thousands of European Jewish children.
7. The correct answer is the National Refugee Service.
8. The United Synagogue of America is closely related to the Jewish Theological Seminary.
9. The second Temple was destroyed in the year 70 C.E. by the Romans.

10. It is the J.W.B. which stands for Jewish Welfare Board (or, more accurately: National Jewish Welfare Board). It is the Jewish group that is part of U.S.O. (United Service Organizations).

11. It is the H.I.A.S. which is the Hebrew Immigrant Aid Society. The more accurate name is Hebrew Sheltering and Immigrant Aid Society. It was created in 1909 by the merger of the Hebrew Sheltering House Association (founded in 1884) and the Hebrew Immigrant Aid Society (founded in 1902).

12. *Yad Va-shem* was established to commemorate the massacre of Jews during the Nazi era.

13. Its English name is Workmen's Circle.

14. These two organizations are part of Reform Judaism and are related to the Union of American Hebrew Congregations.

15. The correct answer is YIVO. In 1956 its English name was changed from Yiddish Scientific Institute to YIVO Institute of Jewish Research.

16. Her name is Henrietta Szold. After the Nazi rise to power, she became the leader of Youth Aliyah which saved many thousands of Jewish boys and girls from extinction in Europe. She was always deeply interested in fostering friendly relationships between the Jews and Arabs of Palestine.

17. His name is Stephen S. Wise. Judah Magnes and Abba Hillel Silver were also rabbis and well known Zionists.

18. The name of the organization is WIZO. The women's Zionist organization counterpart in America is Hadassah.

19. His name is Isaac M. Wise. Jonah B. Wise, also a rabbi, is his son.

20. The correct answer is Reconstructionism.

21. The Samaritans did not accept the teachings of the Talmud as binding, and they did not accept the Bible in its entirety. They accepted only the Pentateuch as the full Bible, and Moses as the only prophet.

22. The largest group that opposed the teachings of the Sadducees was the Pharisees.

23. The Reform group also calls itself Liberal Judaism.

24. They were all presidents of theological seminaries. Of this group only Cyrus Adler was not a rabbi·

25. The Rabbi Isaac Elchanan Theological Seminary is the rabbinical school of Yeshiva University.

26. Max Nordau is best known for his devotion to Zionism. He was one of Herzl's advisers on Zionist problems.

27. This society published old Hebrew books hitherto unprinted.

28. The name of this organization is the American Jewish Congress.

29. The name of the organization is the American Jewish Committee.

30. Bar-Ilan is a university organized under Orthodox auspices.

31. The program is called the Basle Program. Basle is a city in Switzerland.

32. Dr. Samuel Belkin became president of Yeshiva University in 1943. He succeeded Dr. Bernard Revel as president. Dr. Pincus Churgin was dean

of the Teachers' Institute of the same institution for many years.

33. B'nei Akiva is affiliated with *Hapoel Hamizrachi.*

34. The term *Bais Din* (also spelled, Beth Din) is closely related to *Sanhedrin. Bais Din* means court of law. The *Sanhedrin* was a Jewish high tribunal in the post-biblical period.

35. The Bezalel School specializes in teaching arts and crafts.

36. A *Chevra Kadisha* is a group that handles the details of burial.

37. The correct answer is Samaritans and Reconstructionists.

38. It was called the College of Jewish Studies. The other two institutions are not located in Chicago.

39. Morris Raphael Cohen spent the major part of his life teaching at the City College of New York (C.C.N.Y.).

40. The ideas and beliefs of these scholars would fit best with the thinking of Conservative Judaism.

41. The movement is called *Hasidism.*

42. The flag of Israel has a white background with two blue horizontal stripes on either side of the star.

43. The name of the organization was Haganah.

44. The name of the organization is Hadassah.

45. The name of the organization was BILU.

46. Sura and Pumbedita were famous for their great academies.

47. The organization of Menahem Beigin was called the *Irgun.*

48. The group was called the Peel Commission.

49. Haifa has two major universities: Haifa University and the Technion (Israel Institute of Technology). Tel Aviv University is the only major university in Tel Aviv. Bar Ilan University is on the outskirts of Tel Aviv.

PART IV – Bible

Answers to questions on pages 105-150

1. They were accused of being spies.
2. Jacob's new name was Israel.
3. She saw the wicked city of Sodom being destroyed.
4. Noah sent out a raven and a dove.
5. The Bible does *not* say that no prisoners may be taken.
6. Eliezer was the servant, and Rebekah was the girl.
7. Zipporah, Jochebed and Miriam were related to Moses. Zipporah was his wife. Jochebed was his mother. Miriam was his sister.
8. A kosher animal must chew its cud and must have split hooves. Cows and sheep fall into this category; horses and pigs do not.
9. One of Joseph's dreams was that the sun, moon and stars bowed down to him. These represented his father, mother and brothers.
10. The Israelites called this food *manna*.
11. The name of the city set aside for Joseph's father and brothers was Goshen.
12. Dinah and Zipporah, as well as Eve and Ruth were not married to Abraham, Isaac or Jacob. Hagar was married to Abraham, and Rachel to Jacob.

13. Joseph recognized his brothers first. They did not recognize him.

14. Jacob and Esau were the twin sons of Isaac and Rebekah.

15. Aaron, Jethro and Amram were related to Moses. Aaron was his brother. Jethro was his father-in-law. Amram was his father.

16. Chapter 31 in the Book of Proverbs speaks words of praise about the Woman of Valour.

17. This quotation is found in the Book of Psalms, chapter 90.

18. The Latin translation of the Bible is known as the Vulgate.

19. The two tribes were Ephraim and Manasseh. Ephraim and Manasseh were the two sons of Joseph.

20. There are 39 books in the Bible.

21. The king divorced her. Later Esther was chosen queen to replace Vashti.

22. The Tribe of Levi served as priests.

23. The Book of Tobit is part of the Apocrypha.

24. The name of that person was Abraham.

25. Zipporah was the wife of Moses.

26. These words are *urim* and *tumim*.

27. The son was Joseph. He had been sold to a group of Ishmaelites who, in turn, sold him to an Egyptian.

28. Ruth was a Moabitess. She adopted Judaism after her husband, Mahlon, died. She returned to Bethlehem with Naomi, and eventually married Boaz, a relative of Naomi.

29. The fifth book of The Five Scrolls is the Book of Ruth.

30. Saul was David's father-in-law. David had married Michal, Saul's daughter.

31. Akiba is the only one of the five listed who is not mentioned in the Bible. He lived in the post-biblical period.

32. The name of the 50th year is the Jubilee Year.

33. Moses did *not* appear before Pharaoh for forty days and forty nights.

34. The Book of Jeremiah is *not* part of the Torah. The Torah consists of only the first five books of the Bible. The Book of Jeremiah is part of the Prophets.

35. She hid him in a basket among the bulrushes.

36. The Amalekites were very hostile to the Israelites. They blocked the way as the Israelites were marching through the desert towards the Promised Land.

37. Leviticus is not a part of the Prophets. It is part of the Pentateuch (or Torah).

38. Hillel is not mentioned in the Bible. He lived in the talmudic period.

39. Aaron accompanied Moses when he appeared before Pharaoh.

40. Hagar's son was Ishmael.

41. Adam was the first man.

42. The name of the man was Job.

43. Samson said this to Delilah.

44. Samson is the author of this quotation.

45. The name of the fourth matriarch is Leah. Sarah, Rebekah and Rachel are the other three.

46. Ezekiel was not a Minor Prophet.
47. Caterpillars are not referred to in the Ten Plagues.
48. The Levites derived their livelihood from the tithes that were collected.
49. The missing word is "pruning-hooks." The same words appear in the Book of Micah, chapter 4.
50. The two should not be used together.
51. His name was Methuselah.
52. They are the sons of Noah.
53. The book is called the Book of Nehemiah.
54. Persons who took such vows were called Nazirites.
55. Jacob worked for Laban in order to marry Rachel. Laban had fooled Jacob. Originally, he was to work for Rachel for only seven years.
56. Her name was Naomi.
57. The name of the prophet was Nathan.
58. Her name was Zipporah, and her husband's name was Moses.
59. Zelophehad was a member of the tribe of Manasseh. Zelophehad died in the desert leaving five daughters and no sons. Until this time, daughters could not inherit their father's property. But the daughters demanded their father's share in the Promised Land. As a result of their demands, new legislation was proclaimed permitting a daughter to inherit (if there were no sons). If, however, the daughter marries someone who is not a member of her father's tribe, she does not inherit. See: Book of Numbers, chapter 27.

60. Moses is *not* mentioned in the first book of the Bible.

61. It was called The Garden of Eden.

62. Her earlier name was Sarai; it was later changed to Sarah.

63. The tribe was Amalek.

64. Benjamin and Joseph had the same mother. Her name was Rachel.

65. Reuben planned to return and save Joseph from the pit.

66. Joseph demanded that Benjamin (the youngest brother) be brought to Egypt. Joseph and Benjamin were blood brothers. They had the same father and mother.

67. Jacob said it to Rebekah. The hairy man he was referring to was Esau.

68. The other two were Bilhah and Zilpah.

69. Jacob was asked to marry Leah, Rachel's older sister. In order to marry Rachel as well, he had to work for Laban for seven more years.

70. The brothers were Simeon and Levi.

71. He hit the rock with his staff.

72. Jacob gave Joseph a coat of many colors.

73. Jochebed, the mother of Moses, and Miriam, the sister of Moses, played important roles in the life of Moses.

74. Rachel was the mother of Benjamin. Her other son was Joseph.

75. The butler told Pharaoh about Joseph, and Joseph interpreted Pharaoh's dream. Joseph was then appointed assistant to the king.

76. Pharaoh, the King of Egypt, was present.

77. Bezalel was the architect and artist who carried out the task of building the Tabernacle.

78. Gershon and Eliezer were the two sons of Moses and Zipporah.

79. The dream was about seven lean cows and seven fat ones. The lean cows swallowed up the fat ones.

80. Miriam, the sister of Aaron and Moses led the women in dance and song.

81. The plague of the first born, in which the oldest son in every Egyptian household died, was the final plague.

82. God was talking to Abraham.

83. Aaron made the Golden Calf.

84. "Thou shalt not work on the Sabbath" is the correct answer. The commandment pertaining to the Sabbath is the fourth commandment, and begins with the words, "Remember the Sabbath day to keep it holy. . . ."

85. Moses had an unusual experience near a burning bush: the bush burned, but was not consumed.

86. Abraham was the father and Isaac was the son.

87. Noah's three sons were Shem, Ham and Japheth.

88. We see a rainbow of many colors in the sky.

89. Cain answered: "Am I my brother's keeper?"

90. The quotation refers to the story of the Tower of Babel in the Book of Genesis.

91. The serpent tempted Eve to eat of the fruit of the Tree of Knowledge.

92. They began to speak different languages and couldn't understand each other.

93. The more popular name of the Decalogue is the Ten Commandments.

94. The Holy Scriptures is another name for the Bible. The Torah and Prophets are only *part* of the Bible.

95. Moses was *not* the High Priest.

96. Benjamin, because they had the same mother.

97. His name was Potifar, captain of the king's guard.

98. Her name was Miriam.

99. He would surely die.

100. This tradition was known as Masorah.

101. "Thou shalt love thy neighbor as thyself" is the best known verse in this chapter. The other two quotations are not in the Book of Leviticus.

102. Amos was a herdsman and a pruner of sycamore trees.

103. The women gave him their gold jewelry.

104. His name was Abner ben Ner. Joshua and Akiba did not live during the period when Saul or David were kings of Israel.

105. His hair became entangled in a tree, and he was killed as a result.

106. Psalms, Chronicles and Proverbs are part of the Hagiographa. Malachi and Jonah are part of the Prophets.

107. His name was Ahab. Both he and his wife were notoriously evil people.

108. Abigail was originally Nabal's wife. Nabal was a wealthy Calebite who was very rude to David when David asked him for help.

109. Abraham's intended sacrifice of Isaac is known as the *Akeda,* which means the "binding."

110. The Book of Lamentations (called *Echah* or *Aychaw* in Hebrew) is read on Tishah B'Av.

111. They are the names of two cities noted for their wickedness.

112. David was the son of Jesse. He killed his opponent (Goliath) with a slingshot.

113. They are all false. The Bible doesn't say that the fruit Adam and Eve ate was an apple. Jonah was swallowed by a big fish. The Bible doesn't say it was a whale. Esther and Mordecai were cousins.

114. The burning bush burned, but was not consumed.

115. The Song of Songs is also called Canticles.

116. Joseph asked these questions of his brothers.

117. The second time the Ten Commandments appear is in the Book of Deuteronomy, chapter 5, verses 6-18.

118. Christian tradition maintains that the first is not a commandment, and they divide the second into two commandments. There is also a tradition among some Christians that omits the first, and divides the tenth into two parts.

119. The Latin phrase *creatio ex nihilo* means "created out of nothing," and refers to the Story of Creation in the Book of Genesis.

120. The Pilgrims of whom the Bible speaks were those Jews who visited the Temple in Jerusalem during the three major holidays.

121. His name is Elijah.

122. The Hebrew term is *halitzah* (or *chalitzah*).

123. The Greek word is Hagiographa.

124. Hagar was Ishmael's mother.

125. These were the three friends of Job, as described in the Book of Job.

126. The name of this person was Daniel.

127. The name of the judge was Jephthah.

128. Fish must have fins and scales to be kosher.

129. Jacob rolled the stone off the mouth of the well so that Rachel might fetch some water. See chapter 29 in the Book of Genesis.

130. It is located where the Muslim shrine, the Dome of the Rock, is now situated.

131. The sons of Jacob told him that Joseph was devoured by a wild animal when he was actually sold to a band of Ishmaelites. They, in turn, sold him as a slave to the Egyptian Potiphar, captain of Pharaoh's security forces.

132. Moses was so named because he was "drawn forth from the water" when discovered in the bulrushes by the daughter of Pharaoh.

133. Joseph and Daniel were successful in interpreting dreams: Joseph interpreted Pharaoh's dreams and Daniel interpreted the dreams of Nebuchadnezzar, King of Babylonia.

134. The Hebrew names of Daniel's three friends were Hananiah, Mishael, and Azariah.

PART V – Holidays, Laws and Ceremonies

Answers to questions on pages 151-174

1. Lag Ba-Omer is a spring holiday. It occurs on the 33rd day after the second day of Passover, which is the equivalent of the 18th day of the Hebrew month, Iyar. This generally falls during the month of May.

2. *Bedikat chametz* is performed in the evening on the day before Passover.

3. The object is a *mezuzah*.

4. It is permissible, by law, to name a baby after anyone, living or dead. In some communities, however (among Ashkenazim, in particular), it is not customary to name children after living people.

5. These refer to various types of ritual practice, particularly in connection with the prayer service as practiced in various countries.

6. These are all words that refer to Jewish liturgy. A *machzor* is a holiday prayerbook. A *piyyut* is a prayer-poem. *Piyyutim* are found in the *machzorim* used on various holidays. *Amida* is a Hebrew word meaning "standing." It refers to the Silent Devotion which is recited while standing.

7. These are all types of prayerbooks.

8. *Maror,* meaning "bitter herbs," is eaten at the Passover Seder.

9. Rosh Hashanah occurs on the first day of Tishri.

10. The Torah is called the Written Law and the Talmud is called the Oral Law. Originally, the teachings of the Talmud were passed on from generation to generation by word of mouth.

11. *Yaaleh v'yavo* is recited on Rosh Chodesh and holidays. In the Spanish and Yemenite ritual it is also recited during the *Amida* of the *Musaf* service of Rosh Hashanah and Yom Kippur.

12. *Bikur cholim* is a Hebrew phrase meaning "visiting the sick."

13. According to the triennial cycle it took three years to read the entire Torah at the Sabbath service, compared to our one year. This three-year cycle was followed in Palestine as late as the 12th century.

14. It is a reminder of the destruction of the Temple in Jerusalem. A more scientific reason (and probably the original one) is the noise created by the breaking of the glass scares off the evil spirits.

15. More wine is drunk on Passover. Drinking of four cups of wine at the Seder is mandatory.

16. It is performed on the eighth day after the birth of a boy.

17. Israel's independence day is called *Yom Haatzmaut.*

18. The original source of the Hebrew passages found in the *tefilin* are the Book of Exodus (13:1-16) and the Book of Deuteronomy (6:4-9 and 11:13-21). The leather box which is placed on the

head (*shel rosh*) has four compartments, with four strips of parchment on which these four passages are written. The box placed on the arm (*shel yad*), however, has only one compartment, and all four sections are written on one piece of parchment.

19. *Yizkor* is recited on Pesach, Succos and Shavuos, as well as Yom Kippur.

20. It is called Succos, or Tabernacles.

21. We do not eat or drink anything on Yom Kippur.

22. The story of Haman and his plot to destroy the Jews is read on Purim from the Scroll of Esther.

23. Rosh Hashanah, Yom Kippur and Succos all occur during the Hebrew month of Tishri. Purim occurs during the month of Adar.

24. Kosher animals can be eaten only if properly slaughtered, salted and washed off before cooking.

25. Fish can be eaten immediately.

26. The first requirement is that the animal have split hooves and chews its cud.

27. According to Jewish law a person is a Jew if his mother is Jewish, regardless of his father's religion.

28. A *minyan* requires the presence of 10 males over the age of 13.

29. The first day of the Ten Days of Repentance is Rosh Hashanah.

30. Chaim Nachman Bialik, the famous Hebrew poet, conceived the idea for the *Oneg Shabbat*.

31. Another name for Tu Bi-Shevat is Arbor Day.

32. *Shivah* means "seven."

33. Liberty was proclaimed throughout the land to

all the inhabitants. Slaves were freed, but were not given the land on which they worked. All land purchased since the previous Jubilee reverted to its original owner. See Leviticus, chapter 25, for more details.

34. Pesach begins on the fifteenth day of Nissan, and Succos begins on the fifteenth day of Tishri.

35. Chanukah is not mentioned in the Bible. The Bible had already been completed by 165 B.C.E. when the episodes leading up to the holiday takes place.

36. The *lulav, esrog* and *sukkah* are all connected with the Succos holiday.

37. The third holiday, Pentecost, or the Feast of Weeks is called Shavuos in Hebrew. It is so called because it takes place seven weeks after Passover.

38. These are the names of the three daily prayer services.

39. That day was Yom Kippur.

40. On Jewish leap years we add a whole month. The month, Adar II, is added seven times in every 19 years.

41. It takes place on Purim. The term is derived from a rabbinic saying which declares that on Purim one is to be so deleriously happy that he can *hardly tell the difference* (which is what the term means, literally) between the phrases "blessed is Mordecai" and "cursed is Haman." In Israel the carnival usually consists of a parade of decorated floats through the city.

42. She is called an *agunah,* which means "a deserted one."

43. *Al chet* is a prayer of confession recited on Yom Kippur.

44. *Tishah B'av* is like Yom Kippur, in that both are observed as fast days.

45. A *Baal Koray* reads the Torah at public services.

46. The ceremony is called *tashlich* and is observed on the afternoon of the first day of Rosh Hashanah. If the first day is Sabbath, it is observed on the second day of Rosh Hashanah.

47. The long gown is called a *kaftan*.

48. The full Hebrew phrase for circumcision is *b'rith milah*.

49. These are all various types of food.

50. These all refer to types of articles that are worn by men or women. The *sheitel* is a wig worn by women. The *shtreimel* is a type of hat, and the *gartel* is a belt worn by men (usually *chassidim*).

51. *Moaz Tzur* is sung on Chanukah, after lighting the candles.

52. The ceremony is called *havdalah*, which means "separation" (separating the holy day from the week days).

53. On holidays that fall on week days five *aliyos* are distributed. On Yom Kippur six *aliyos* are given out.

54. The Nazirites and the Rechabites refrained from drinking wine.

55. The *Mezuzah* is placed on the upper section of the right doorpost, as one enters the room.

56. Abraham found a ram to use as a substitute when he was about to sacrifice his son, Isaac.

57. The Kol Nidre is recited only on Yom Kippur, at the evening service.

58. The *lulav* is called a palm branch.

59. This can take place at any time when the Torah is read.

60. Although there is no prohibition against eating blintzes on Purim, traditionally they are eaten on Shavuos. Hamantaschen is the special delicacy associated with Purim.

61. The fourth letter is a *shin*. The letters stand for the four Hebrew words, *nes, gadol, hayah, shom,* meaning "a great miracle occurred there."

62. The Megillah is read at the evening *and* morning service.

63. A grogger is used to make noise.

64. The special dessert is called *afikomon.* The word is derived from the Greek, meaning "dessert."

65. It is read on Shavuos, because it is the holiday on which the Jews accepted the Torah (and so did Ruth). The phrase, *zeman matan toratenu* (the time of the giving of the Torah) is used in connection with Shavuos.

66. The holiday is Chamishah Asar Bi-Shevat, and occurs on the 15th day of Shevat.

67. The *talis* and *arba kanfos* must have *tzitzis* (fringes) on them to be kosher.

68. Chad Gadyo is the last song of the Passover Seder.

69. The Hebrew word for canopy is *chupah.*

70. These words are all used in connection with the *bris* (circumcision) ceremony. The *Mohel* performs the circumcision. The *Sandek* is the godfather. He holds the child during the ceremony.

Among East European Jews the *Sandek* is given two assistants, a man and a woman. The man is called, *K'vater*, and the woman *K'vaterin*. Their task is to take the child from the mother and to bring him to the *Sandek*. Today these are purely honorary and symbolic functions.

71. These words are associated with the Succos holiday. *Hadasim* (myrtle branches) and *Aravos* (willow branches) are used with the *Lulav*. *S'chach* is the covering of leaves or branches placed on the roof of the *Sukkah*. The *Pitom* is the pointed stem at the tip of the Esrog.

72. One of the requirements for conversion is to be immersed in a *mikveh*, which is any kind of body of natural water (a lake, an ocean, etc. . .). The other ritual requirement for males is that they be circumcised.

73. The partition is called a *mechitza*.

74. In the early history of the Jewish people the Sanhedrin was the body that enacted laws.

75. Joshua and Gideon used the shofar to overcome the enemies of the Jewish people. Joshua used *shofrot* (plural of *shofar)* to bring down the walls of Jericho, and Gideon, one of Israel's judges and heroes, sent the enemy into confusion by having each member of his select army of 300 all blow on *shofrot* as they attacked.

76. The Purim holiday is celebrated during the Hebrew month named Adar.

PART VI–Art, Entertainment and Sports

Answers to questions on pages 175-200

1. The player's name is Andy Cohen. He replaced Rogers Hornsby in 1928 as the Giant second baseman, but did not become an outstanding attraction as expected.
2. Charles "Buddy" Myer won the batting crown in 1935.
3. The name of the actress is Gertrude Berg, known as Molly Goldberg in the popular radio and TV productions. She died in 1966.
4. His name is Al Jolson.
5. His real name is Nat Holman.
6. The name of the play is *Abie's Irish Rose.*
7. Louis "Satchmo" Armstrong is a convert. He is the second well-known Negro in show business to convert. Sammy Davis Jr. is likewise a convert.
8. His name is Lucius N. Littauer.
9. It was called the Maccabiad.
10. His real name is Al Schacht.
11. The composer's name is Sigmund Romberg.
12. His name is Adolph Zukor.
13. Maxie Rosenblum's nickname is Slapsie Maxie.
14. Her name is Sophie Tucker.
15. He was an umpire.
16. His name is Richard Tucker.

17. His name is Arthur Szyk.
18. His name is Steve Lawrence, husband of Eydie Gormé. They met on the Steve Allen Tonight show.
19. It is the story of the painter, Vincent Van Gogh.
20. His name is Sid Luckman.
21. His name is Jacob Steinhardt.
22. Maurice Schwartz is the famous Yiddish actor.
23. Her name is Hepzibah.
24. Sid Gordon is one of the few players in baseball to perform this feat.
25. The Marx brothers were a comedy team.
26. Benny Friedman played for the University of Michigan. Later, he played professionally for the New York Giants.
27. The family name of these stars was Adler.
28. Abe Saperstein's team is called the Harlem Globetrotters.
29. His name is Barney Ross.
30. His name is Artur Rubinstein. He began his career at the age of 12.
31. Her name is Sarah Bernhardt.
32. His name is Leonard Bernstein.
33. Their names are Dick Savitt and Herb Flam.
34. Ernest Bloch was a composer of Jewish music. His works include *Israel* symphony, *America* symphony, and *Shelomoh,* a rhapsody for cello and orchestra. His *Avodat Ha-Kodesh,* a Sabbath service, was first performed in 1934.
35. Daniel Mendoza was a boxer.
36. Edward Israel Iskowitz was Eddie Cantor's real name.

37. Marc Chagall created the stained-glass windows at Hadassah Medical Center.
38. Samuel Reshevsky was an outstanding chess player. He began his career in Poland as a boy wonder and later settled in the United States.
39. The family name is Damrosch.
40. The sport they played was soccer.
41. Jascha Heifetz is one of the world's greatest violinists.
42. His name is Johnny Kling. He played for many teams, but won distinction during the time he played for the Chicago Cubs.
43. The name of the composer is George Gershwin.
44. His name is Arthur Miller.
45. Lipman E. Pike was the first professional baseball player.
46. Fanny Brice created Baby Snooks.
47. It is called Habimah.
48. His name is Jacob Epstein.
49. His real name is Henry.
50. They were all cantors. Richard Tucker later became an opera singer.
51. They are all tenors.
52. His name is Sid Gillman.
53. They are all Yemenite singers of Hebrew folk songs.
54. His name is Max Baer.
55. Jan Peerce also excels as a cantor.
56. Gottlieb and Henshel made their reputations in basketball. Eddie Gottlieb played for, managed and owned the Philadelphia Warriors at various points in his career. Henshel was prominent in

amateur athletics. He managed the 92nd Street
YMHA basketball team at one point. He gained
real prominence as a member of the U.S. Olympic
Basketball Committee on which he served from its
inception until his death in 1936.

57. Rudy Larusso played for Dartmouth from 1957-59.
His full name is Rudolph Anton Larusso. Later,
he played professionally for Minneapolis and Los
Angeles. Art Heyman played for Duke, and Barry
Kramer played for N.Y.U.

58. Abe Segal, whose full name is Abraham Alan
Segal, won the South African national singles
championship in 1964. Cal Abrams was a baseball
player who played for many National and American League teams from 1949 to 1956. Vic (Victor)
Hershkowitz has won more than 30 national cham-
pionships in handball, after winning his first title
in 1947.

59. The name of this outstanding coach is Red Auerbach. His team was the Boston Celtics. Auerbach
retired as coach in 1966. Mel Allen is not a player.
He was a radio and TV announcer for the N.Y.
Yankee games for many years. Sarachek has been
coach of the Yeshiva University basketball team
since 1943.

60. The sport is Ice Hockey. The award is known as
the National League's Hart Trophy Award. It was
donated by Hart's father, Dr. David A. Hart,
during the 1923-24 season.

61. His name is Mike Epstein. In the Minor Leagues he
played for Rochester. In the Major Leagues he played
for Baltimore.

62. Elizabeth Taylor was converted to Judaism.
63. Sammy Davis, Jr., the black entertainer, was converted to Judaism.
64. Rod Carew, an outstanding black major league baseball player, married a Jewish girl and converted to Judaism.
65. The Orte Wingate School is Israel's famous school specializing in physical education. It was named after a British general who was a friend of the Jewish people.
66. Mark Spitz is a swimmer.
67. All served as cantors at High Holiday services, but only Richard Tucker and Yossele Rosenblatt served as full-time cantors in a congregation. Tucker and Peerce were opera singers; Rosenblatt never was.